8 |

100 IDEAS
30 R ESSENTIAL TEACHING SKILLS

11 A

21 FEE
- 4 JU

0 8 MA

1 4 0C

WITHDRAWN

BF

Books
Books
All boo

CONTINUUM ONE HUNDREDS SERIES

100 IDEAS
FOR ESSENTIAL
TEACHING
SKILLS

Neal Watkin and Johannes Ahrenfelt

BLOOMSBURY
LONDON · BERLIN · NEW YORK · SYDNEY

Published 2013 by Continuum
an imprint of Bloomsbury Publishing Plc
50 Bedford Square, London W1B 3DP

www.bloomsbury.com

ISBN: 9780826491565 (paperback)

A CIP record for this publication is available from the British Library.

Typeset by Ben Cracknell Studios
Printed and bound in Great Britain

This book is produced using paper that is made from wood grown
in managed, sustainable forests. It is natural, renewable and
recyclable. The logging and manufacturing processes conform
to the environmental regulations of the country of origin.

CONTENTS

SECTION 5 Transform Your Teaching to Meet Pupil Needs

SECTION 6 Move Your Pupils On

SECTION 7 Working With Your Pupils

SECTION 8 Bring Order to Your Teaching Life

Focus your Teaching

You will hear these words uttered in most staffrooms, usually by dishevelled veterans worn down by years of government initiatives. We are not suggesting that you become cynical and bitter, but we are saying that the question is a powerful one and needs to be rescued from these people and used extensively.

Every lesson we teach must have a point. It is easy to become dependent on specifications and the National Curriculum for our rationale, or to deliver a lesson because it appears in the departmental scheme. If the only reason you can find to teach a particular lesson is that the pupils need to know the content, then there is little point in carrying it through: the chances are that it will be flat and lack rigour, and it will run the risk of producing behaviour problems in the pupils and poor quality learning. However, if the teacher can walk into the classroom and say, 'Today, we are going to develop your communication skills', or aim to make them more responsible citizens by developing their understanding of a key social concept, then something important has been achieved. The 'point' of the lesson will drive it forward; it will give focus to the activities and provide the teacher with a logical and meaningful plenary.

There are several ways to make a lesson worthwhile:

O Develop or assess a particular skill.
O Provide an overview for a series of lessons.
O Draw links between various elements at the end of a unit.

These should always be considered before content. Information is the raw material that will allow pupils to create or improve something, it is not an end product in itself. So, when you have created a lesson plan, ask yourself what pupils will get out of it; how will it help to move them on?

The job title 'teacher' implies a flow of information from an expert (you) to a grateful recipient (the pupil). This is the traditional view of the teacher, where chalk and talk holds sway and the teacher says and the pupil does.

However, the focus of the profession is shifting. The emphasis is no longer solely placed on what teachers do, but takes into account what pupils get out of the lesson. This is a view shared by Ofsted and most educational theorists. There needs to be a balance between planning your interaction and looking at what pupils will do and how they will do it.

One way through this is to think of yourself as an assistant to learning. In your lesson, the pupils are in control of a process that will allow them to reach a specific goal, and your job is to question them in order to steer them in the right direction. Pupils then become the central focus of the lesson: what they achieve is more important than the style, delivery or work rate of the teacher. Think about the following:

O Have a point to your lesson (see Idea 1).
O Get pupils active as soon as possible.
O Instruct the whole class for no more than 8 minutes at a time.
O Maximize pupil talk time by providing well-structured group tasks.
O Allow pupils time to show what they have learned during a lesson.

This is not to suggest that the role of the teacher is unimportant. The teacher is a key ingredient in pupil learning, but he or she must work with the learner in an equal partnership.

Lessons can take pupils in a number of directions. To simplify matters, we could split these into two categories: 'thinking' lessons and 'doing' lessons. Of course, all activities and lessons will involve an element of thought and also some need for action: but it is essential to recognize the focus of your lesson. Will you decide to make pupils think about a topic or skill, and draw conclusions about it? Or will you challenge them to put skills and knowledge into practice?

Both of these approaches are valid and should be used in conjunction with each other over a series of lessons. For example:

LESSON 1 (DOING)

When introducing a new topic, you might give pupils a set of cards containing stimulus material and get them to categorize it in a number of different ways.

LESSON 2 (DOING)

In this lesson you might get pupils to produce a piece of display work on a specific part of the work, adding to their existing knowledge. They could use the information to design the overall look of the classroom wall display, as well as their individual piece within it.

LESSON 3 (THINKING)

Now that the knowledge has been firmly embedded through a series of 'doing' lessons, you can get the pupils to think about the information they have learned. Ask them to reflect on the role of the topic studied within its wider context, or to predict the next step or consequence. You might want to compare it to a previous topic and draw out similarities and differences.

The benefits of 'doing' activities are that they allow pupils to feel the information or topic and learn in an enjoyable and active way. 'Thinking' lessons allow the information to be taken into new areas and established within the context of the pupil's learning (see Idea 12).

Giving your lesson a multi-sensory overhaul has many benefits. You will make it more interesting and therefore hook pupils, but you are also more likely to hit on a style that each member of the class is happy with and can relate to quite easily. This will increase participation and interest and therefore improve results.

The traditional style of lesson introduction would usually involve the teacher standing at the board to lay out a few basic bits of information and give the instructions and parameters of the task. Use visual, audio and kinaesthetic methods together in an introduction, and the experience is transformed from a passive activity into something engaging and memorable. Having your pupils focused at the beginning of a lesson is vital if it is going to succeed.

You might have a maths lesson in which pupils are learning to interpret the shape of graphs. The title could be 'When is water not water?', and pupils will explore the cooling rate of ice. Possible visuals could include images of water and ice (or real examples, if you are feeling brave), and the essential of a completed graph. The audio input would come from the teacher explaining the features of a graph and pointing them out. It would also be heard when the teacher explains the purpose of the activity and the outcomes of the lesson. Kinaesthetic learning could take the form of a card sort, that gets pupils to identify the key features of a successful graph and then add them to a diagram to label it.

The same principle can be employed with main activities. If a unit involves 12 lessons, try to have four that have a visual activity, four that involve large amounts of listening and speaking, and four that involve movement and manipulation (or 'practicals', as the scientists call them).

ADDRESS LEARNING STYLES

Pupils have a preferred way of establishing patterns and sequences. Teachers must be aware that our tendency is to present information in its verbal form. This will work for some pupils, but others will struggle to engage (see Idea 4). For this reason, many researchers have mapped out the ways in which pupils learn so that teachers might match the content of a lesson to the preferred style of their audience. The most widely known of these is Gardner's 'Multiple Intelligence' theory.

The chart opposite looks at Gardner's eight intelligences and suggests some activity types that support them.

Learning styles and multiple intelligences have been popular and used widely in schools. Recently, however, there have been articles criticizing labelling of children and trying to teach them in their preferred style.

A sensible approach is to make sure that your lessons have variety. During a sequence of lessons, make sure that you cover all the styles. Testing for learning styles is fun and can give a boost to lessons: just ensure that pupils go on to experience a number of styles and are asked to become rounded learners. They need to explore in order to find their unique balance.

Multiple Intelligence	Activities
Visual-spatial	○ Using graphs, maps and diagrams ○ Creating posters or leaflets
Linguistic	○ Debating and discussing in groups or pairs ○ Actively using words through writing essays or poems
Bodily-kinaesthetic	○ Using role play and drama to explain ○ Learning through field trips and visits
Logical-mathematical	○ Completing problem-solving activities ○ Trying to find patterns
Musical	○ Producing songs about a topic ○ Analysing music and interpreting it
Interpersonal	○ Working as part of a team or pair ○ Teaching others
Intrapersonal	○ Researching a topic individually ○ Self-evaluation and setting of targets
Naturalistic	○ Learning through observation and experimentation ○ Collecting data and categorizing it

It is important to know what type of lesson you want to teach. This will inform your planning and help you set objectives. Below is an outline of three very different approaches. You can either see which is most suited to your personality and develop that strand, or try to teach a mixture of all three in order to give your students variety.

SEMINARS

The seminar approach requires some preparation. It relies on the pupils preparing material at home and being ready for the lesson. The activities can then focus on finding patterns in the knowledge and developing links. An example of this type of approach is the classic lesson, 'the great balloon debate'.

The benefit of this approach is that pupils have good background on which to base ideas and there can be more of a focus on exciting activities.

WORKSHOPS

In this type of lesson pupils will learn new information by doing a series of activities. The learning will be active and hands-on. It could involve card sorts or interpreting data – any activity that gets pupils handling information or objects.

This can be an exciting way of working, with pupils discovering new things. They should come away from the lesson feeling that they have really learned.

LEARNING MYSTERIES

The third style involves the teacher not revealing objectives. Instead, they inform pupils that they will have to come up with an explanation as to why the lesson is important, and how it fits in with the general topic being studied.

The benefit here is that pupils are focused on the purpose of the lesson. They will come away really knowing why this was an important lesson.

Having a style is important, but so is giving pupils variety. Finding the balance will be one of problems you need to solve.

Can you envisage a situation where a task is set (for example, 'Produce a piece of audio-visual media that explains the rock cycle and create an A4 revision guide on the topic') and then pupils move into groups and begin to research and respond creatively?

There are two main reasons why pupils find it hard to work independently:

○ Many pupils need spoon-feeding. They cannot seem to get on unless the steps that need to be taken are clearly laid out.
○ Many teachers believe they are under pressure to deliver content and so revert to a style of teaching that minimizes thinking and maximizes output.

Instead, give pupils an end product to work towards, and explain that the purpose is for them to solve problems independently. Share with them the skills you want to see improving. Try the following approach:

1 Allow pupils to choose their own groups (of three to five people). You could teach them about group dynamics, roles and gender.
2 Let pupils give their group a name, which should be relevant to the task or situation. This encourages them to reach decisions collectively.
3 Make sure pupils are aware of the outcomes. It is important that they are not stranded.
4 Pupils must establish their own procedures. Stress how vital planning is, but don't do it for them. They should aim to have 15 to 20 ideas before they begin. Plans should be displayed.
5 The role of the teacher is to keep the momentum going in each group. Ask questions: 'Tell me about . . .'.
6 Have regular reflection sessions. Think how much time you would spend in a normal lesson on review/consolidation. Model a criteria reflection session.

This approach needs to be fully debriefed with pupils.

THINK ABOUT INDEPENDENT LEARNING

USE KEY QUESTIONS AND ENQUIRY QUESTIONS

Questions are the weapons of choice for teachers. We can use them to keep control, gauge understanding, develop a theme and build confidence. Questions can create a positive atmosphere and offer helpful guidance to pupils.

It makes a lot of sense to turn your whole lesson into a question. First, it gives you and the pupils a focus. What is expected becomes clear and students are helped to make sense of the activities. Effective learning is about making links between a number of different pieces of information (think about the various parts of a lesson: starter; introduction; task; development activity; plenary) and a question gives you a cohesive way through the learning and helps to bring disparate elements together.

Second, a question helps with engagement. If there is a question then there has to be an answer, and whether they want to or not, pupils will get that momentary flicker in their minds. If you capture their imagination with a good enquiry question then you have a head start on behaviour and progression.

The question should be open and interesting, and involve an element of investigation. For example, a Languages lesson that was looking at the words for foods and shops might be entitled 'How could you impress Thierry Henry?'. The teacher could explain that Thierry has gone home to Les Ulis, Paris, for his birthday. You need to buy him a present and cook him a meal. This might link a starter using pictures of food, with a map exercise and shopping vocabulary and even linking words such as 'firstly' and 'after that'.

The appeal is obvious, but the real benefit comes in giving the lesson purpose. The skills are brought to the front and the transferability of the content is easily seen.

Knowing what you want to achieve over a series of lessons is vital in order to focus yourself and pupils. For example, teaching *The Canterbury Tales* because it is there in the stock cupboard is not reason enough – that will not make it relevant in the classroom. You could not walk into a Year 8 set and tell them that Chaucer is important and that they simply need to know about it. You need to devise a route through the work that concentrates on a single aim and a set of skills. Continuing with the same theme, we might have an enquiry question that asks, 'How relevant is Chaucer in the 21st Century?'

Having a question is important. It will immediately encourage pupils to engage with the material in this unit and provide a goal to achieve. Beyond this, the task will need breaking down into a number of smaller areas of study, each accompanied by a question. This will allow pupils to explore the topic and see that a complex answer is required. We should not dumb down and make everything completely straightforward – accessibility is crucial, but all pupils in all sets need and like rigour. So, the unit might contain the following:

Week 1: *Who was Chaucer?*
Why did he write The Canterbury Tales*?*

Week 2: *What messages do the tales contain?*

Week 3: *How could the tales be updated for a modern audience?*

Week 4: *Has morality changed since medieval times? What issues are important to people today?*

Week 5: *How would you tell the stories in a twenty-first century set of tales? What would they say?*

Week 6: *How relevant is Chaucer in the twenty-first century? How would you justify this to TV executives?*

Making the aims explicit at the beginning establishes clear criteria for success and brings confidence and motivation.

WRITE 'SCHEMES OF LEARNING'

Ideas 8 and 9 set out a clear philosophy for planning. This should form the basis of a scheme of work. Begin by having the overview in front. You might consider using this as an introduction and reference guide for staff: a front sheet, if you like, that sets down the questions and the key skills covered.

The next step is to work out what should be included in each individual lesson. QCA recommend that the information for each lesson should be split into four sections.

Calling the finished document a 'Scheme of Work' suggests an activity that has to be done, a task that must be done in order to complete a process, something to fill the time. If we instead talk about a 'Scheme of Learning', then we are putting skills at the forefront and developing the idea of interaction with students, involving them in the process and allowing them to go on a journey. We provide the road maps, but the direction must be their own (see Idea 11).

Learning objectives	Possible teaching activities	Learning outcomes	Points to note
Pupils should learn:		*Pupils:*	
Lesson question?			
This column contains the key knowledge and understanding that pupils will learn during the lesson. It is best displayed as bullet points.	Starter: Introduction: New learning/ introduction of task: Development: Plenary: (See Chapter Two of this book formore explanation and ideas)	Outline the subject specific skills that will be learned or developed within the context of the lesson. (The shading indicates the importance of this column)	The last column gives you an opportunity to make links to previous learning, list resources, or share vital with the other teachers who will be using the scheme

HOW TO ENSURE PUPIL PROGRESSION

Moving pupils on with each lesson you teach might seem like a daunting prospect, but there are ways to focus your teaching and ease the strain.

Before you start to plan, identify several skills that you want to develop within your lessons. Planning is a whole lot easier if you do this before establishing content. Look at the example opposite. It shows one skill can be built on across a unit of work in Year 7 History:

The first column acts as a benchmark – a basic requirement that all pupils should meet. This can be practised and expanded upon in the lessons that follow. Study the 'communication' row. Here, the basic requirement is that pupils should be able to work effectively in groups. This is something that should have been established in the previous unit, but a quick activity where pupils negotiate and set out class rules for group work should reinforce the desired approach. In the next session, where the skill is tackled, pupils will have to consider various options and then reach a joint conclusion. This marks significant progress within and between lessons.

This technique speeds up planning. If Lesson 4 in the scheme is about how castles developed over time and how they were used to control people, then a task that gets pupils to create a wall display using set resources will achieve your skill objective. The task is an obvious choice for the purpose – no more sleepless nights thinking about the right activity!

Progression chart

Britain 1066–1500

Skills		PROGRESS IN HISTORICAL SKILLS		
	Lesson 4	**Lesson 6**	**Lesson 8**	**Lesson 12**
Communication	Cooperate with others to produce work	Debate points and negotiate to reach conclusions	Offer advice on improvement using criteria	Produce an argument that everyone agrees on

Progression within lessons and across an academic year is easier to plan for and record if the teacher possesses some sort of reference point.

Bloom's Taxonomy can be that tool. It consists of six levels of thinking and allows pupils and teachers to see how thinking and work become more complex and therefore demands greater mental effort. It shows how progression can be achieved and provides an easy reference point for the 'next step' approach to teaching and target setting (see Idea 59).

The chart below shows the levels of thinking and suggests question starts and prompts that cold be used to gain answers at each level.

Evaluation	*To what extent . . .*
	How important is . . .
	Convince someone . . .
Synthesis	*Create a . . .*
	What conclusions can you make?
	What would happen if you changed . . . ?
Analysis	*What evidence is there to support that view?*
	Compare and contrast . . .
	What patterns emerge?
Application	*Can you put this information into categories?*
	Can you give an example of that?
	Demonstrate how to . . .
Comprehension	*Can you describe a . . . ?*
	In less than 30 words, tell me about . . .
	Explain your findings to your partner.
Knowledge	*Who discovered . . . ?*
	Go to the library and research . . .
	Label the diagram.

If these are displayed within the teaching room, then pupils can also use them, identify the level of their own thinking and move themselves on. Bloom's Taxonomy provides a focus for what is required within the classroom, both for staff and pupils. Teachers should aim to ask some high order questions within a lesson, and pupils should aim to answer some.

Design Challenging Lessons

STARTERS: POST-IT!

Grab their attention immediately and turn your first five minutes into a quick-fire activity, while you are taking the register or simply want them engaged instantly – it's Post-it time!

POST-IT!

At the start of the lesson, have Post-it notes on their desks ready for when they come in. While you take the register, ask them to write down three things they remember from last lesson. When you have finished taking the register, ask for suggestions.

POST-IT AGAIN!

Stand by the door and give pupils a Post-it note as they enter the room. Ask them to write down a key word/sentence/fact, etc. that they remember from last lesson. When they have finished, ask them to place the notes on the board and read out one of their suggestions (you may have to choose a selection of pupils rather than the whole class).

POST-IT MORE!

You have written down a name/verb/place/year/etc on Post-it notes. Pupils place these on their foreheads without looking at them (this is crucial!). In pairs, pupils ask the other person yes and no questions which guide them to the item on their foreheads. For example, a pupil might have the word 'Shakespeare' on his or her note and so has to ask questions such as 'Is he alive?', 'Is he famous?' etc.

POST-IT OUTLAW!

One pupil describes a key word to the class without using any of the 'outlawed words' on the Post-it. The class tries to guess the key word.

Using Post-it notes gives the pupils immediate focus as they enter the room and also encourages them to get involved in the lesson. It only takes a couple of lessons before the pupils get used to the routine when these little 'stickies' are handed out.

If you haven't yet invested in a class set of this excellent resource, then now would be a good time to do so. They serve as a great tool for checking understanding instantly and the whole class is involved – both sitting and standing!

READY, STEADY, ANSWER
The class writes down one-word or symbol answers and then shows the teacher. Pupils could also be encouraged to explain their answers.

VOTING
The teacher gives the class options to choose from and the pupils then have to vote on the option they consider to be the most suitable. They then stand up so that the teacher and the class can spot the disparity between choices/options.

DRAFTING
Pupils use their boards to draft answers which could be fed back verbally. Alternatively, they could write down three key things from the last lesson (as in Idea 13), especially if the whiteboards are to be used frequently in the lesson.

REVISION AND PAIR WORK
Whiteboards serve as perfect flash cards for testing vital information, and without the need for cutting out hundreds of cards! The teacher could provide one pupil with a list of various facts, such as key words, mathematical problems or simply a set of pictures. The other pupil has to write the correct definition/answer on their board, which they show their partner.

This activity is ideal to check immediate understanding, and gives the teacher the possibility to scan the classroom quickly for potential problems in learning. It also stimulates those kinaesthetic learners who sometimes find it difficult to focus for longer periods of time.

STARTERS: MINI WHITEBOARDS

Entice your class with this varied and fun activity using a range of audio-visual tools. The only thing the class has to do is to give it a name!

PICTURES

Either have a picture on the board/OHP or have them on pupils' desks ready for action. Ask the class to come up and name the picture or write a small caption. Another idea could to be for the class to add speech bubbles next to the picture.

MUSIC AND SPEECH

Play a piece of music or speech as the class enters the room. The pupils give the piece a title relating to its content and have to give reasons for their choices.

VIDEO CLIPS

Pupils watch a brief clip related to the lesson and write their own subtitles – with sometimes hilarious consequences! Alternatively, they give the clip a title or name (mini-whiteboards could be used here, see Idea 14).

TEXT

Have a piece of text on the interactive whiteboard/OHP or on separate pieces of paper on pupils' desks. Ask the class to decide on a title for the text. It could also be a good idea to ask them to decide on its origin, background and authorship. Alternatively, use the text to form the basis for the content of the lesson – can any of them guess the theme/content of the lesson?

This starter lends itself well to all subjects, as it is easily modified and varied. The activity can also be used to test pupils' prior knowledge and understanding and encourages them to use their imagination and wit, and will stimulate their wider understanding of the topic.

Encouraging pupils to talk, and especially to each other, about the subject can sometimes be challenging. The following activities are excellent for this purpose and can be used as a main activity, hook or starter to get the class thinking about a particular issue or task.

THE SECRET BAG GAME

Choose your mystery object and place it inside a bag – old sacks or bags made out of material is recommended above plastic carrier bags, to create a more mysterious atmosphere. Ask a pupil to come to the front and place their hand inside the bag. They then have to describe the content to the rest of the class who will attempt to guess its content. Adding some atmospheric music or even sound effects can add more excitement to the task.

THE TORCH

Switch the light off and try to get it as dark as you possibly can. With a torch in your hand, place the mystery object on the desk and shine the light on it a little at a time. Each time ask your intrigued audience for suggestions about what the object might be – the stranger the object the better the activity.

THE SECRET PATH

Place a number of items on the floor of the classroom. If possible, try to scatter them around the room and near the pupils. Using a torch (or why not add more excitement by using a candle?), walk along the path and shine your light in front of you. Ask a few pupils to follow you and explain what they can see.

Using objects in this way gives pupils the opportunity to enhance their communication skills and creates a stimulating learning environment, in which the class can work together to find out what the mysterious object might be.

Turn your class into directors and producers in this enjoyable and stimulating activity. It is time for Music, Camera, Action!

Choose a group of three to four pupils to come to the front of the class. Explain that the class are about to listen to a piece of music and that the group should use their imagination as well as their understanding of the topic to act out a brief scene based on what they have heard. The scene can contain dialogue, but using only motion is preferable. The rest of the class act as directors and can ask the actors to 'freeze' in a certain place in order to ask what they are doing/feeling.

Another alternative to this activity could be to use digital cameras or camcorders to capture each segment or scene, and analyse it together as a class. This footage could also be used as a starter for the next lesson or as plenary during the one in progress.

To develop this idea further, ask another group of pupils to play the role of scriptwriter or journalist by asking them to write a brief script based on the scene. This would turn this small activity into a main task, and a piece of homework could also be set for next lesson or as preparation for this one. For example, a scene could be prepared before the lesson and the rest of the class has to guess what the scene is about/what the music is referring to, etc.

This task is a great way of challenging your class to use their imagination as well as their knowledge and understanding of the subject or topic.

The idea behind this lesson is to encourage communication and get pupils thinking on their feet. By moving around the room from station to station pupils are having to refocus their attention regularly, and will naturally cooperate with each other as time is a crucial factor. 'Class: get ready for Action Stations!'

Set up a number of work stations for groups of three to four (preferably no bigger), and place a number of sources of information in the middle. These could be everything from photographs, text or textiles to laptops and televisions. Ensure that each station has something different on it so that this activity really becomes action-packed! One way of making it more exciting could be to conceal the items where possible and ask the pupils to reveal them only when the timer or music starts. Set a time limit which cannot be altered, for example seven minutes, and set them to work. Pupils move to the next station when the music stops. When each group has been to all stations, ask them to sit down where they are standing. Go through the task with the class.

Action Stations is a fantastic activity which pupils enjoy. It is relatively easy to set up and a perfect tool to really challenge that hard-working class of yours!

ACTION STATIONS!

THINK/PAIR/SHARE

This is a really effective way of building up the levels of discussion and the quality of answers in the classroom. It will help pupils to avoid giving one-word answers and start to create more developed responses.

STEP ONE – THINK

Give all pupils in the room a piece of stimulus material and an open question. Allow pupils time to look at the material and then five minutes to write down as many points as they can. It can useful to set a minimum level: explain to pupils that the best ideas are not always the first ones to come to mind, and that a range of suggestions will create a better answer.

STEP TWO – PAIR

Once everyone has a set of ideas, ask them to move into pairs. Each pupil should talk through their points with their partner. Next, the pair should create an answer that both people agree on. Stress to them the importance of cooperation and why it is better to look at all the ideas before making a final decision.

STEP THREE – SHARE

Finally, pupils can share their work with a wider audience. You might decide to do this as a whole-class discussion, or create groups of four to six pupils. Everyone should now feel confident enough to contribute. The ideas have already been tried and tested on two levels and so the possibility (in pupils' minds) of 'getting it wrong' and looking foolish is eradicated.

Think/pair/share can be modified and become useful when deconstructing text and for general assessment for learning work. Pupils become confident at evaluating exemplar work and interpreting criteria.

This is a difficult task for many teachers and one that needs particular attention. Try these quick-fire ideas and hopefully they will be asking you for more!

IT'S IN THE VOICE

If you want them to get stuck into a piece of writing quickly, ask them to spot what dialect or accent the person has who is writing. Then why not ask a brave soul to read the text in that particular dialect/accent to get a feel for the text?

IT'S IN THE LANGUAGE

Place a number of Post-it notes around the room – on walls, under desks and in filing cabinets. Inform the class that they have to solve a mystery which has been written on the board. The mystery could be the key question of the lesson, or a problem that they have to crack. In pairs, pupils begin looking for the clues scattered around the room, and take notes/gather data using their books or mini whiteboards (see Idea 14). End the activity by asking for feedback from a few of the pairs.

IT'S IN THEIR HANDS

This activity requires the pupils to write quickly and think on their feet. Split the class into groups of three or four. Explain to the groups that they are about to receive information and they have to compile enough writing for another group to be able to understand it. The catch is that each member of the group can only write one word each before passing it to the next person, so communication is crucial. Read them a short story or a set of instructions, etc. Then play a piece of music, and when it stops each group passes their answer to another group, who then reads it to see if it makes sense.

Remember writing those short stories when you were younger where you wrote one sentence at a time and then passed it on to the next person, and then found the final story absolutely ridiculous? This activity is similar except, this one makes sense!

At the end of the lesson, ask pupils to spend 30 seconds thinking about what they have learnt either in this or in a series of lessons. Then, starting in one corner of the class, ask a pupil to mention one thing that they can remember. The pupil standing to their right then has to think of something that links with the last comment. The person standing next to them continues doing the same thing, until the class has exhausted the topic or the last pupil has spoken.

'That links to . . .' is a fantastic way of challenging pupils to think about the bigger picture and how things link together, and to encourage them not only to focus on what they have grasped in one lesson or in one activity. This plenary is also excellent for revision.

Do pupils really understand the purpose of your lessons? Can they see how the aims and objectives were met and why – and at what point? Could they explain to you what the aims were at the end of a lesson? This short plenary gives you the opportunity to see if they have understood.

At the end of the lesson, ask the class to spend one minute writing down what they think the aim of the lesson was – what was the point of it? Initially let them do the talking, but if they find it difficult guide them if necessary by giving them clues about the module as a whole and what you have been looking at in this particular lesson. It does not mean they have not grasped the purpose of what you have been teaching them. They are merely not used to this kind of question. When the aim has been identified, try asking them if they can think of why they study this particular unit in your subject, and what they can gain from it.

If you use this plenary regularly, it enables the pupils to get used to this type of question and helps them see the bigger picture. Suddenly whole modules or units seem to make more sense to them and they become more involved. Some topics are easier than others, but if they never understand why your subject is important then what is the point?

PLENARIES: SOLVING THE LEARNING MYSTERY

Encouraging movement during the last few minutes of the lesson is a great way of creating a mental note in the pupils' minds that you can refer to in the following lesson – memory flashback.

MOVE!

This activity starts with the pupils standing behind their chairs. Pupils move to a choice of three: Middle, Left or Right side of the classroom, based on the possible answers to the key question of the lesson. Pupils then have to explain and give reasons for their choices. It also gives the rest of the class an idea of the various options available. Great opportunity for whole-class feedback.

MOVE AGAIN!

This version requires the pupils either to remain standing or sit down, depending on what the teacher asks them about. The final question will generally leave only a handful of pupils standing.

Ask pupils to stand up behind their chairs. Inform the class to 'Remain standing if . . .' you have ever owned a pair of shoes, for example. After each question a number of pupils will sit down. This activity is great way of making pupils understand something through using themselves as visual tools.

MOVE MORE!

The class organizes themselves in lines, rows or groups, based on, for example, chronological order, thematic order, to complete a sentence, irregular and regular verbs, nouns, pronouns, etc. The teacher then asks the class to reorganize themselves based on a set of criteria. Setting a time limit to the task is also an effective way of making them focus quickly.

These activities will encourage pupils to collaborate to solve a task, as well as think on their feet with little or no help from their teacher. Move! is also structured so that all pupils will be able to take part during much of the task.

Getting pupils to talk can sometimes be difficult. Getting some pupils to focus their talking is difficult too. This short activity will hopefully help those shy ones and chatterboxes to contribute more effectively.

The two-minute talk is as simple as it states: a talk that lasts for no longer than two minutes. The good thing about this easy task is that even if the child has to stand in front of the class, they know it is only for a very short period of time. The other beneficial part of this is that the more confident pupil who could potentially spend the entire lesson talking about something will learn to be more concise as you, the teacher, will stop them after exactly two minutes.

The two-minute talk can be used for all year groups, even adults, and is an incredibly easy tool to practise public speaking and remaining succinct.

PLENARIES: TWO-MINUTE TALK

Deliver Razor-Sharp Lessons

BEGIN WITH A STORY USING VISUAL AIDS

It has been widely reported that pupils pay most attention at the beginning and end of a lesson. Therefore, it is worth spending time planning carefully for these episodes. Having a memorable starter will help to engage pupils and put them in the right frame of mind for the rest of the lesson.

Having a multi-sensory starter is good for a number of reasons (see Idea 13), but a powerful one is that pupils will be engaging more than one sense. Telling a brief story at the beginning of the lesson will provide a clear example of what you will be talking about and show pupils how ideas and concepts can link together.

TEACHER AS STORYTELLER
Prepare a series of visual images and a short script so that you can relate a story about an event or happening. Have the images on display so that you can point to them, or use PowerPoint to make them appear on screen at the right time. This can be done with people (Rosa Parks for Civil Rights), imaginary characters (a raindrop for the water cycle), or symbols (the journey of x in a simultaneous equation).

TEACHER AS HI-TECH STORYTELLER
It is really easy to create small animations using the timer on PowerPoint, with the pages like frames on an animation camera. Motion paths are also useful.

PUPILS AS STORYTELLERS
Put up an image or series of images and ask pupils what they think is happening. If there is some ambiguity or essential background information, then this works much better. For example, the Loan execution photograph from the Vietnam War depicts a dramatic scene. Although initial sympathy lies with the victim, knowing the context and his past deeds makes passing judgement much more difficult.

No sane person would begin a car journey without a vague notion of where they were heading. Apply the same principle to lessons and allow yourself a few minutes in the introduction to discuss with pupils where the learning will take them. This could happen in several stages:

O Discuss the lesson question and its meaning, and collect some initial thoughts or guesses. This will generate thinking and engage pupils with the lesson content.

O Provide the scaffolding (supporting questions) and say you will be asking these at various intervals throughout the lesson. Planning and displaying your questioning for pupils is a good technique for widening the amount of pupils who contribute to group discussions

O Share the objectives and skills that will be developed. Say to the class, 'By the end of this lesson you will have . . .'. This alerts pupils to the key components and flags up what they should be spending the majority of their time developing.

O Model any end products that you wish the group to produce. This will raise expectations and give pupils a visual reference point while they are working.

If the pupils are not surprised by the content of the lesson, then there will be less misunderstanding and greater participation.

SEEING THE END BEFORE THE BEGINNING

A short and incisive role play can invigorate a lesson and inject some humour into the proceedings. It can also give pupils a visual representation of key components, and this can aid memory and help to cement learning.

THE HAPPENING OR SEQUENCE ROLE PLAY

This is useful if you are trying to explain a phenomena or action where components have specific roles that are repeated. Assign pupils to perform a certain role, or something to symbolize it (a simple, but carefully chosen, hand gesture will do), and then read out the sequence and event and let the pupils play their parts. Discuss afterwards as a class.

For linear structures, you can ask several pupils to come to the front and give them identity cards. They must order themselves so that the structure is correct and then read out the cards to the class. Again, this should be debriefed as a class.

THE SCRIPTED ROLE PLAY

If you are about to teach a difficult topic, with multiple events and/or characters, then a scripted role play could be an alternative. The teacher prepares a series of cards to be read out. Several pupils are told to wait outside. The class are instructed to react in a certain way after every speech. Possibly, have the audience in character and reacting in different ways.

For example, you could have a role play about the differing opinions and political stances concerning stem cell research. Pupils can take on the speeches as campaigners, doctors and politicians. The audience can be split into various groups and react with a thumbs up or down and a mild 'yes' or 'no' as each speech is given.

If pupils come away knowing that it is a complex issue and there are many opinions, then the overview has served its purpose.

Teachers want pupils to produce work in a variety of genres. It is important that pupils experience different types of writing and get a mixed diet of computer work, verbal presentation and written activities. To take this work a step further, teachers can explore the genre with pupils and the differences between different types of text.

Pupils are often set the task of producing a newspaper front page, mainly because it feels a little more exciting than the phrase, 'Write an essay on the title . . .'. However, there is an opportunity here to complete some meaningful literacy work and to explore convention with pupils.

Start with a blank newspaper front page and ask pupils what features all newspapers have in common. They will immediately come up with headlines, a title, images, captions and so on. Extend their thinking and ask them why these are included. Explore the size of text and placement of images.

If you want to take this further you could use the 5Ws (see Idea 51) and get pupils to write the first paragraph of their story in less than 35 words. This will sharpen their skills of selection and make them explore the concept of relevance.

In the plenary, pupils need to be given time to link up the work they have done and apply it to other areas. The teacher must help them recognize the skills they have used and explain why literacy is not just something they will encounter in English.

TIME KEEPING

Keeping the pace (see Idea 46) and keeping to set deadlines within the lesson is crucial for a good lesson. Read these simple hints and see if they help.

HINT 1

Make sure pupils are always aware of timings. This can easily be achieved using a visible clock such as the 'clock tool', which you can find in most Interactive Whiteboard software.

HINT 2

Give the class deadlines which mean something to them. Informing someone that you will be back in a 'tick' does not indicate what time you will return. The same thing goes with children: telling them that they have to complete a task does not really mean anything to them. If, however, you inform pupils that they have 'six and a half minutes' to complete their work, it makes more sense to them. They can look at the clock and make a judgement about what needs to be done.

HINT 3

Record different pieces of music with various time lengths and store them either on the local network or on CD so they can be accessed easily. Instead of using the clock, just play, for example, track number four, which is exactly six and a half minutes long. Inform them that they have six and a half minutes and that when the music stops the time is up.

Timings can be difficult to stick to, especially if you have a lot to get through in a lesson. Using tools such as music really does help both the pupils' learning and your own time keeping.

Keeping pace is a real skill and one which we all try to perfect. Try these ideas and see if they can help you as much as it has us!

THEY KNOW WHAT YOU ARE UP TO . . .

Set clear aims and refer to them regularly in the lesson: this way you can tick or cross these off as you go along or when you do mid-lesson reviews. Try to have a list of what is coming next so that pupils have an idea where they are, what to expect, and even when the homework is going to be set, so that the momentum of the lesson is kept at all times.

THEY KNOW WHEN THE TIME IS UP . . .

Use short, reachable deadlines and make sure they know what these are (see Idea 45).

THEY KNOW THE QUESTION . . .

Try informing pupils that you are going to ask them a question about a particular issue in a certain time, for example two minutes. This technique is useful for those quiet children or those who need 'thinking time'.

THEY KNOW THE GAME . . .

Limit dead time by keeping pupils occupied between main tasks. This can be achieved by asking them to formulate an answer, or note down things they can see in an image while you are handing out resources.

These quick ideas are easy to implement and can naturally become part of your everyday teaching. Each time you try something that aids pace in the lesson, write it down for future use.

MAKE TRANSITIONS SMOOTH

An excellent lesson will have a starter, main activities, homework, plenary and lots of learning. Ensuring that these components follow on from each other smoothly can be difficult. Think about these hints and it will be easier!

ROUTINE

Get into an easy routine so that your pupils know what to expect at the start of every lesson. For example, have a small note on your wall explaining that they are to write down three things they did in the lesson before in the back of their books while you take the register or hand out resources.

THE BEGINNING

Make sure that your starter naturally leads into the lesson: the register can be taken later on while they are working.

FLEXIBILITY

If pupils are working well but have not finished the task at the time your lesson plans states, allow them to complete. If you stop them while they are actually producing good work, the lesson can become fragmented and the class may not get a sense of closure or understand coming activities.

THE END

Make sure that your plenary checks or consolidates their learning, and finish the task before the bell goes. If you can dismiss them calmly after the plenary, the next lesson will run even smoother as they get used to working, without having to wait or be disrupted.

What did *you* think of the lesson? If you felt stressed and rushed then the children might have felt the same, and little or no learning may have taken place. It is difficult not to push them into the next task, as planning takes time and we all want them to learn as much as possible. If they complete one task, well they have gained much more and you have yet another excellent lesson in your bag!

Starters and plenaries get a lot of press, but splitting the main body of your lesson into smaller parts will give you the space to explore ideas in greater depth and significantly move forward the learning of pupils.

Assume that a basic lesson has the following episodes:

O Starter
O Introduction
O Activities
O Homework
O Plenary

There is an opportunity to add an extra step and reinforce key concepts as well as give opportunities for assessment and progression. Take the 'activities' episode of the lesson and divide it into two parts: new learning and development.

The 'new learning' section will allow pupils to engage with new material and start to make sense of it. It is their opportunity to discuss and sort knowledge, and build up a mental picture of the topic.

This is followed by the 'development' activity. The purpose is to demonstrate what they have learned and use it in some way. This can be as simple or as complex as you desire, but the idea is that some sort of check is given regarding the learning. It could be a written activity that you mark later, or it could be the production of a mind map in small groups which is then shown to the rest of the class.

Not only does this give the teacher more scope within a lesson, but it connects the learning in a more effective way:

O Starter – engages the pupil and introduces the main theme/skill.
O Introduction – gives the big picture and expectations.
O New information – allows pupils to gain knowledge on a new topic.
O Development – the learning is demonstrated and checked.
O Homework – the learning is extended or linked to the next lesson.
O Plenary – all learning is reviewed, including processes and where else it can be applied.

ADDING A DEVELOPMENT ACTIVITY

Engage Your Pupils

HOOK THEM: MUSIC AND IMAGES

Using music and pictures in your teaching is always a good idea, especially as it provides diversity and can stimulate pupils in a different way than text does. Try these ideas and see how they can hook the most challenging pupils!

ZEN OR EXPRESS TRAIN

Try using music to excite or calm a class, even if it is at the beginning of a lesson. If you know that your pupils have high energy levels and sometimes need to calm down, play some tranquil music as they come in. They may find it strange in the beginning, but they get used to it quickly. With your sleepy GCSE class, try putting some of their favourite tunes on as they come into the room or even while they work. It will raise their energy levels.

PAINT THAT TUNE

Place chairs in a large circle. Decide on a piece of music that is relevant to your lesson. Give each pupil a sheet of paper and some pencils, and inform them that they can draw whatever comes into their heads about what the lesson might contain. Stop the music after about 30 seconds. They stop drawing and pass their masterpieces to the person to the left of them. Play the music again and they continue with the drawing the person next to them started. Do this at 30-second intervals until the music has finished. At the end of this activity, each pupil will have a picture to which all of them contributed.

These short activities really work well with all classes and subjects. Music on its own can change the atmosphere in the room within seconds, and if you then add an opportunity for them to show off their artistic flare, then you are on to a winner.

This is a really simple way to involve the entire class in a recap activity, and also to motivate them for the rest of the lesson. It is loosely based on the old TV show *What's My Line?* and makes pupils ask questions and think about the implications of answers. They will have to make links and create a mental picture of a given topic.

Ask for three volunteers and then send them out of the room. Write the numbers 1, 2 and 3 on the board and ask pupils to nominate three people, concepts, or items that were important in the previous lesson (for example, characters from a novel; fractions; chemicals with different reactions). Assign one of the three identities to each number (without displaying them) and then invite the volunteers back in the room and get them to stand beneath a number. Next, ask the class to stand up.

Each volunteer now asks a 'yes' or 'no' question to a classmate in order to work out who or what they are. When a person has answered a question they sit down. If the guessers identify themselves before all the class has answered then they win, but if there are no more classmates to ask then they are defeated. It is important to state clearly that they are only allowed one direct guess: 'Am I . . .'

This 'hook' can be repeated at intervals to allow all pupils to be the ones at the front. It is a particularly effective way to begin lessons on questioning, planning, and character profiles, or when identifying properties/ key features.

How do we create a sense of curiosity about the subject that we teach, and what is the most effective way to get pupils interested quickly? Enter Shock Tactics!

MAKE THEM UNSURE

The class enters a dark room (or as dark as possible) with loud music playing as they sit down. To spice things up a little bit, have an image on the Interactive Whiteboard or OHP with a question above it, for example: 'Why did he do it?' or 'Is this the man?' Imagination is everything!

CHANGE WHAT THEY KNOW

Change the layout of the classroom entirely by moving desks, books and chairs. For example, move your desk to the other side of the room.

CONFUSE THEM

Ask a pupil the lesson before to teach the first 15 minutes of the next lesson, or as long as you deem appropriate. When the pupils enter the room they will find a fellow classmate writing on your board and welcoming them into the room as you would do. You could walk in after the class and sit where the teacher/pupil would normally sit.

The idea of gaining pupils' attention, interest and curiosity at the start of the lesson with an intriguing image, story, analogy or puzzle has long been used by teachers. Trying something drastic can sometimes be an effective way into a lesson, as it provides immediate stimulus as pupils enter the room and they become curious about what the lesson might cover.

Lessons that begin in a mysterious way can often prove to be exciting and mentally stimulating. The desired effect is creating a willingness to engage with the material, and leaving the pupils wanting more.

Putting the lesson title into a coded sequence and having the pupils work out the meaning is one way to grab their attention.

PICTURE CODES

Substitute the words in the title for images, or sequences of images. For example, the word 'see' could be represented by an illustration of water (the sea!), and the word 'category' might be seen as a kitten (cat) + a luggage tag (tag) + a bloody scene from a vampire film (gory). A Native American saying 'hello' is a good representation of the word 'how' and if your question starts with 'which' there is an obvious alternative.

This becomes even more effective if the lesson is about interpreting data or inferring from information.

LANGUAGE CODES

Sometimes, writing the title in a foreign language and having the pupils work out what it says based on patterns and words they think they know can be an interesting starting point. German throws up lots of possibilities and is easy to find words that resemble their English counterpart. Obviously, this lacks the impact in German lessons!

Alternatively, use a grammar or word rule to establish a pattern. For example, capital letters that are used incorrectly within a passage could spell out the title.

A small prize for the fastest pair in the class is guaranteed to put pupils on task and engage them.

HOOK THEM: DECODING

Thinking skills lessons are excellent tools for engagement. Pupils like to be challenged and they like to be active. Thinking skills lessons that focus on active learning in groups generate ideas and extend thinking beyond the normal level you could expect from a group.

In order to plan a good thinking skills activity, you need to decide where it should be pitched. Research has shown that effective learners are the pupils who can take new knowledge and categorize it, before adding it to their already acquired knowledge. Therefore, if you want a good thinking lesson, you must find a topic in which pupils have some background knowledge. It might, therefore, be ideal to place such a lesson near the beginning of a unit, so that pupils can begin to see what the topic is about without acquiring too much knowledge for it to become stale regurgitation.

Quality thinking takes place in the grey area between what pupils definitely know and what they cannot comprehend. You want to include an element of surprise so that pupils are made to think about its connections and significance, but they also need somewhere to pin this knowledge.

So, you might have begun a unit about blood. You have taught two very exciting lessons about the role and functions of the heart. You might, at this stage, split the class into groups of three to five and give them the question, 'Why was Billy the blood cell lying helplessly in a bathroom sink?' The groups could be given a set of 24 statements and asked to come up with an answer.

Some of the cards would contain statements about the heart, some would cover the other parts of the body involve in the journey, and some would cover the immediate circumstances that led to Billy's predicament.

A major reason why thinking skills activities work so well is that they utilize both long- and short-term memory. A good activity will ask pupils to process some information quickly, but then build on that by using knowledge they already possess.

ODD ONE OUT

This is a simple activity to get pupils thinking about key words within a topic. You need to construct a grid with 30 words from the unit being taught, for example:

1.	2.	3. sugar	4.	5.
6.	7.	8.	9.	10.
11. butter	12.	13.	14.	15.
16.	17. cheese	18.	19.	20.
21.	22. flour	23. raisin	24.	25.
26.	27.	28.	29. cream	30.

These words are placed in sets of three, and pupils have to say which of them is the odd one out. It is important that the words are displayed in the format below:

Set A:	*11.*	*22.*	*29.*
Set B:	*3.*	*17.*	*23.*

It would be easier to give pupils sets of three words instead of numbers, but this would not get them actively using their short-term memory. By providing them with numbers you will be making them look at the grid to find the words and this will access short-term memory.

Once they have discovered the words in the grid and written them down, they can start to decide which word is the 'Odd One Out'. The activity is more effective if the pupils stress what the two remaining words have in common: for example, Cheese is the odd one out because butter and flour are both ingredients in pastry.

For another example, see Idea 34 (Who Am I?). You can apply the principle of long- and short-term memory to any activity. It will require thought about layout or sequence, but it is worth the effort.

MAKE THE THINKING VISIBLE

Part of the problem with getting pupils to think is that it is not tangible. Thinking can be shown to pupils so that they can see how it is developing, and once it is fully down on paper and out in the open they can start to analyse it. It is at this point that pupils will start to see links and connections that they could not have made in their heads. Making the thinking visible also helps with long-term memory, and is therefore good for revision.

CONCEPT MAPS

Linking together factors and causes of reactions is not always easy for pupils. If the task is broken down so that one link is created at a time, the process becomes much easier to comprehend. Try putting a question in the middle of a page and surrounding it with nine boxes containing nine prompt words or phrases. Give pupils the sheet and ask them draw a line between two prompt boxes that link together. They should then explain the link by writing along the line. Encourage pupils to find as many links as they can – this will be enhanced if pupils are in groups and discussing the work.

Once complete, the concept map can provide a starting point for the planning of written work. Pupils will be able to see the links and create factors and themes for themselves. The visual nature of the activity is helping pupils to see the 'big picture'.

A key part of any thinking skills lesson is the debrief. It is a kind of plenary, but contains several important elements for extending thinking, consolidating the learning and making it transferable.

EXPLAIN THE ANSWER IN DEPTH

It is important that pupils talk through the answers they have come up with and explain them fully. They will have spent time working towards this answer and so should be given the opportunity to deliver it. If they do this at length, they will be improving their explanation skills and learning to draw on their work as a source of information.

WHAT WERE YOU THINKING?

Question pupils about the thoughts they had as they were completing the activity. What made them arrive at the answer they did? Was there a moment when it all started to fall into place?

EXPLORE PROCESSES AND TECHNIQUES

A key part of the debrief is talking over what techniques were used to arrive at the answer. It will take a few attempts for pupils to get this right, but when they do the group can really start to explore what needs to be done in order to achieve certain tasks.

WHERE ELSE CAN THIS BE USED?

If we can help pupils to connect the learning in this lesson to another context, their thinking will really improve. Ask them if there were activities before this one where they could have used the same techniques. Extend this to other subjects, or the world outside school and help them to make the skills really transferable.

DEBRIEF PUPIL THINKING

MIND GAMES

Memory, or committing things to it, is a major part of school life. Pupils will need to memorize information in preparation for exams and assessments, so it should be part of our responsibility to help them see how the memory might be improved and what techniques may prove useful in different circumstances.

MYSTERY IMAGE

Place an image related to the topic outside the room or under cover on the teacher's desk. Inform the pupils that they should look at the image for 20 seconds and then try to reproduce it on a piece of paper. During their 20 seconds they must work without the aid of pen or paper – this is a memory exercise. The pupils will work in groups, but will be called out individually.

Divide the pupils into groups of four and ask them to devise a strategy for the group, on what should be recorded and how it will be achieved. Also, ask them to think about how the group will function and how they can help each other to succeed. Give them an idea of what they will be drawing, but keep it to one or two words and be vague, 'a map', 'a body part'.

Next, the pupils come out one by one and observe the image. Each pupil returns to the group and draws what they have remembered. When all four members have been up and drawn, the finished pieces can be displayed on the board.

This will need debriefing so that the techniques used for helping pupils remember can be analysed. This can easily be linked to revision strategies and general life skills. The importance of decoding an image can be discussed, both as an exam tool and as another form of literacy.

The curriculum can become very fragmented for pupils, and issues of progression and transfer can be clouded. The lessons you teach need to have some common strands running through them. This is clearly done through a scheme of work, where a sequence of lessons is built around a central topic. The pupils can therefore see how the learning connects, especially if your introductions to lessons refer back to the last lesson.

But, what about the links between schemes? How do pupils make sense of Year 8, for instance? There are ways to achieve this.

BIG QUESTIONS AND LINKING UNITS

As suggested in Section 1 (especially Ideas 8–10), basing your work around questions is a good way to engage pupils: but it also gives them something to hang new information on. If the unit has a focus question then each lesson can feed into that.

If all the units in a school year are connected by a single question, then pupils will see even more purpose in their study. All the units can end up discussing the relevance of the topic to the year question. Put a copy of the question on display as a constant reminder and reference.

PICK A THEME OF CONCEPT

There may be a topic you study that has input into or consequences for many others. Consider integrating this into the other schemes as a single lesson, or as small blocks of lessons throughout a key stage. Have a display board in the room connected to the theme and get pupils to add to it as the work progresses. If they revisit this theme in every unit, through every year they will begin to see how your subject fits together. They may even be encouraged to make other links. This works equally well with abstract concepts, such as justice.

Finding stimulating and engaging revision activities can be difficult. The following activities work wonders with pupils of all abilities.

GET THEM TO CREATE RESOURCES

Split the class into groups of two or three and assign a topic from your unit to each. Then allocate the groups with an end product, for example, a mind map, fact sheet, graph or table. Explain that they are to create a small revision pack that others will be able to use. When the resources have been produced, you could copy them onto one A4 piece of paper. Alternatively, a revision booklet or poster that can be distributed to the rest of the class.

THE GAME MASTER AND THE CONTESTANT

Create cards containing topics that pupils have to revise. Each card has a word, event, topic etc. on one side, and information about that particular word or event on the other. Try to have each piece of information as separate sentences. Hand the Game Master a card and ask them to test the Contestant on the chosen topic, crossing off each piece of information they mention. Set a time limit and play music which creates tension – why not use music from a popular quiz show?

THROW THE CUDDLY TOY

Have your back against the class and inform them that whoever catches the cuddly toy has to answer a question or explain something. Then throw – it's always caught, believe it or not, and the cuddlier the better! An alternative could be to get the pupil who answered the question to come up and throw it in the next round.

Revision is about the same whatever you do with your class, but creating fun and invigorating tasks really does create a stimulating learning environment. Moving away from the traditional methods is always appreciated.

How can you reach the pupils that would rather spend their time in front of the computer instead of writing that essay? Get them involved online by creating your own 'blog'.

WHAT IS A 'BLOG'?

A 'blog', or weblog, is fundamentally an on-line journal. The activity of updating your blog is 'blogging' and someone who keeps a blog is a 'blogger'. Blogs are updated frequently, even daily, using software that allows people with little or no technical background to update and maintain it. They can be as varied and well-sourced as traditional journalism, but they have the immediacy of talk radio.

HOW COULD I USE IT?

The best way of using a blog is as a learning diary, allowing students to log into your blog to view information about your lessons and use links to extension activities. Perhaps the best thing about blogging is the opportunity for pupils and parents/ governors to find out about teaching and, most importantly, about you as a teacher. You decide the content and pupils leave comments or request additional support. The last issue is perfect for those pupils who find it difficult to approach you after the lesson to ask for help.

HOW DO I GET ONE?

You can either buy the software needed or download a free one such as Wordpress from www.wordpress.org. This software will do pretty much anything you need for your blog, and even password-protect areas or particular articles/comments.

Creating a personalized online community for your classes is not only fun but also very rewarding for both the pupils, who benefit greatly, and also for your professional development, as it encourages you to think more creatively about how you use ICT in your subject.

CREATE A 'VIRTUAL' COMMUNITY

We have all seen them: slides full of text, but with animation galore with swishes, whooshes and machine gun effects every second. We have probably all fallen into the trap of adding lots 'because it means that it must be an excellent presentation'! Try these easy-to-use ideas and your presentations will be even more effective than before.

AVOIDING 'DEATH BY POWERPOINT'

Instead of adding lots of text, use bullet points and talk around the topic. Try keeping to about four points per slide. Also, by drawing a rectangle or circle round a word, right-clicking and choosing Order, then Send to Back, you have created a clear highlight which helps to bring out key points very effectively.

KNOW WHERE YOU ARE

If you need to go back six slides quickly without 'rewinding' the slideshow, simply type in the number of the slide you want to return to and press enter. If you need to do this it is handy to have a copy of the slides. You can print out a mini version of the presentation by going to the Outline View and collapsing the details for each slide (there is a button on the left side of the screen in this View that will do this). Then choose to print the outline view.

DON'T LET THEM SEE IT

Sometimes you want the pupils to focus on you and not the amazing slideshow. Simply press the B key on the keyboard and the screen goes black. Press the B key again and the screen returns. If you want to use a white image instead of a black image, press the W key each time.

PowerPoint can be a fantastic tool if used effectively. Simply playing around with it will give you even better ideas!

This tool has become very popular recently, and is a great way of encouraging interaction and hands-on learning. Try out these easy-to-use tips.

BACKGROUND

Use background colours other than white – pastel colours can help improve readability. If you have a problem with glare (from windows, for example), try using various colour combinations, such as a black background with white or yellow text.

INTERACTION

Shapes such as circles or squares can help you create interactive exercises. Squares can act as 'containers' for pictures or words, and circles can provide a focal point for dragging words or pictures. Being able to move items on screen allows pupils to carry out certain tasks, such as matching, re-ordering or categorizing.

An example of a 'drag and drop' activity for Modern Foreign Languages could be to have a picture of a house in the middle of the whiteboard. Pupils then have to drag the correct French word to the correct area of the house. All subjects can create similar activities with this simple feature.

SPOTLIGHTS AND BLINDS

Good interactive whiteboard software will have these tools available. The spotlight tool is excellent for showing only small parts of an image or text, and can serve as a great starter or plenary.

The blind tool creates a black frame across the whole screen, like a blind, which you then can use to hide a section of the screen. The blind can be dragged from all sides of the screen and is fantastic for keeping the pupils focused on a particular section.

These quick ideas are only a starting point to using the Interactive Whiteboard effectively, but can be adapted to create a vast number of challenging tasks for your classes.

USE THE INTERACTIVE WHITEBOARD EFFECTIVELY

BUILD A SIMPLE AND INTERACTIVE WEBSITE

First of all don't worry – this can be achieved with little effort, all you need is a good idea! You do not need to know any computing language, but you do need some basic software, much of which you can download free of charge. If you cannot find any that you like, use a word processor and save your work as a 'webpage'.

KEEP IT SMALL

Use an easy-to-read font such as Times New Roman and try to keep text size 12–14. Always choose smaller pictures above large ones as there are still plenty of people without broadband and massive loading times are annoying. Alternatively, have a welcome screen where users can choose between two sites depending on their connection speed.

KEEP IT INTERACTIVE

Stay away from static pages: get the visitor involved in your site. This can easily be achieved by using hyperlinks to different pages. Everything from quizzes to mysteries can be created using either text or picture links – imagination is everything!

KEEP IT STIMULATING

If you add an enquiry/investigation into the site which you briefly explain on the main page, then the site instantly becomes more engaging and the pupils want to find out more.

KEEP IT AT THEIR LEVEL

Adding large paragraphs of text is neither pleasing to the eye nor pupil friendly, so pitch it right: use short, concise paragraphs and try adding pictures or graphs to explain bigger points of interest.

Creating websites is about the same thing as a good lesson: careful planning. Write down what you want to achieve with the site, whether it's a place to upload your resources or somewhere pupils can find out about lessons and latest school news – then start your masterpiece!

Instead of asking your children to write that termly essay or prepare their poster presentations, ask them to produce a short film to which they can add narration, text, images and video effects.

STEP 1 – STORYBOARD

Get the pupils to storyboard their ideas on an A3 piece of paper with brief explanations of shots, scenes and content. Then ensure that they have a script ready to use – research time!

STEP 2 – FILMING

First, when beginning filming make them know that the film should not exceed three minutes. Keeping it short and snappy is not only good practice, but it also teaches them to be concise and focus on the task at hand. Second, depending on the project or film, try to limit filming to one to two lessons. Even if they do not finish their storyboard, the last couple of scenes can easily be replaced with pictures, music and good narration.

STEP 3 – EDITING

There are several excellent free video editing programs, such as Moviemaker (Windows XP) or iMovie (Apple). Encourage your pupils to create a film which has a good mix of video sequences, text (such as headings and subtitles), music, and some effects and transitions.

STEP 4 – FINISHING TOUCHES

Remind them to answer the question and complete the task. It is easy to get so involved in the editing side of filming, especially arguing about what effect they are to use, that the aim of the task is lost!

Using digital video is a fantastic tool for engaging pupils, and at the same time it teaches them to work collaboratively, write concisely and broaden their creative minds.

CREATE AND USE DIGITAL VIDEO FOOTAGE

Transform Your Teaching To Meet Pupil Needs

Having a question for your lesson immediately prompts pupils to answer it. If you select the right kind of question, they will be drawn into the lesson because they are intrigued and want to find out the answer.

Choosing a question that is right for your lesson is crucial. Certain questions will help to develop certain skills. For example, if you want pupils to draw on many different sources of information and develop a complex answer, then a 'why' or a 'what happened to . . .' question is probably best. For example:

Why did Angie Merton develop a rash over coffee?
Why did Piers have a day off work in 1086?

In both these lessons, pupils would be asked to develop an explanation by using several sources of information. Engagement levels will be high, because pupils will want to know the answer.

With the question and objectives clearly displayed the lesson can begin.

○ **Starter.** Engage pupils with a quick activity that relates to the key skill – a categorization or investigation type of exercise works well.

○ **Introduction.** Go through the objectives of the lesson and share expectations. Show how this activity will develop their skills and where it fits into the topic being studied.

○ **New learning.** In small groups, give pupils range of information. This can be delivered in a structured way involving demonstration and teacher input, or given to pupils as a categorization activity

○ **Development.** Pupils use their newly acquired knowledge to construct an answer to the question. This will involve decision-making, cooperation and pattern-finding

○ **Plenary.** Discuss the techniques pupils used to arrive at their answers and the processes they went through. Sample pupil answers and then refer back to and review the objectives.

This provides a context to help pupils make sense of the information presented to them.

Questioning is vital to pupil progression and to enhance understanding. This is a vast topic, and one characterized by a lot of instinctive practice. Here are some key areas that could be used to improve questioning and therefore understanding and engagement in the classroom.

CREATING KNOWLEDGE TO DEVELOP HIGHER-ORDER RESPONSES

Blasting in with a big open question can be intimidating. Sometimes pupils need to experience the confidence of a few right answers and hear some key words before they are ready to move on.

O Start with description questions.
O 'What can we see?'
O 'What information is this giving us?'
O Move on to explore the information.
O 'Why it is like that?'
O 'What components might be found in similar types of information?'
O Then try to analyse.
O 'What are the similarities and differences?'
O 'What is the real message here?'
O End with a high-order question.
O 'What conclusions can you draw?'
O 'Which is the most important? Why?'

PROBING

Once a response has been given to your question, the interaction does not need to stop. Pupils need to be comfortable with giving lengthy answers, and so you might need to ask follow-up questions to get to the level of answer you desire. Phrases like 'Can you explain that?', or simply 'Carry on', can be really powerful.

USE THE 'NO HANDS' APPROACH

Ensuring that lots of pupils contribute to question sessions is difficult if the same people always raise their hands. Try the 'no hands' approach, and state clearly that after asking a question you will wait a few seconds and then choose someone to give a response. This increases engagement and is more inclusive. It must be coupled with the rule that it is acceptable to say 'I am not sure' if nothing comes to mind.

Research has shown that only one question per lesson comes from pupils – and this will more than likely be to do with procedures rather than learning. Try an activity at the beginning of an enquiry to get pupils asking questions and then discovering the answers.

JOURNALIST'S PAD

Introduce the activity by saying that pupils are going to work like journalists and try to get the real story about an event. Give a very brief outline or scenario and then ask pupils to generate questions they would like to ask in order to gain a full understanding of the situation. Using the five 'W' words as prompts is a good way in who, what, where, when and why. Once pupils have their questions, the information can be given and pupils jot down the answers in note form. Getting them to summarize the entire story in less than 40 words is an excellent (and very journalistic) way to end the task.

HOT SEATING

This is a good technique if you are about to give lots of information about a significant individual, or if it involves a scenario slightly unfamiliar to pupils. A Spanish lesson that follows pupils learning how to describe their town might be followed up with the following activity: explain to the class that they are about to have a visitor from Salamanca. Say that they need to ask questions to find out about the person and the city in which they live. Pupils can then work in pairs to generate ideas and practice pronunciation.

Leave the room and come back wearing a few comedy props. Sit in the middle of the pupils and allow them to ask their questions.

End the activity by producing a tourist web page for Salamanca.

Getting pupils to respond effectively can be very difficult. Teachers have to deal with insufficient answers and under-performing students. To combat this, plan to develop pupil response as it is being produced, rather than dealing with it once the end product has been realized.

RULE 1 – ESTABLISH CLEAR CRITERIA
There is always a reason for an activity, so share it with the pupils. Tell them what skills you will be looking at and set a clear timescale.

RULE 2 – PURPOSE AND AUDIENCE
There are eight recognized types of text to help establish purpose:

- Instruction
- To recount
- Explanation/description
- To inform
- Persuasion
- Discussion
- Analysis
- Evaluation

Also, make sure pupils are aware of the audience. Knowing there is a real audience is also a great motivator.

RULE 3 – MODEL AND DEMONSTRATE
Show pupils a finished product that has the presentation and content levels that you expect from them. Do a mock layout on the board and involve pupils in labelling its characteristics.

RULE 4 – USE ACTIVE LEARNING TO ESTABLISH CONTENT
Construct a card sort activity that will assist with sorting and categorization of relevant information. Throw in a few red herrings to complicate the task.

RULE 5 – ALLOW PUPILS TO PLAN COLLABORATIVELY
Pupil talk will help the flow of ideas and produce better plans. This will allow pupils to feel more secure about the task.

DEVELOP PUPIL RESPONSE

RULE 6 – REDRAFTING

When tackling big assignments, responses will benefit from redrafting. Peer assessment and target-setting are really effective tools for achieving successful redrafting (see Idea 63).

RULE 7 – GIVE QUICK FEEDBACK AND REFLECTION TIME

In your marking, ask pupils a question that aims to enhance their work, such as 'Why is this approach better than the alternatives?' Get them to respond to this immediately.

Differentiation has always been a hard issue for teachers to get to grips with. The aim is to find work and targets appropriate for each individual without causing divisions and resentment within the class.

If you do have classes with a wide range of ability, it is important to plan different activities and have some learners working towards slightly different aims. It is inevitable that some pupils will want to know why they are being given work that is not the same as the rest of the group, so you need to have an answer ready.

First, you need to make sure that all pupils in the room are aware of where you are heading, known in education as the 'big picture'. If they are aware of the lesson question, the unit question and the final piece of work that they will be asked to do, they will be more ready to accept work that helps them move towards that goal.

This allows the teacher to respond to pupils by saying the work they have been given is the 'next step' they need to take in order to work towards the goal. Once this work is done and discussed, they can move on.

Trying to hide the fact that some pupils are doing a different activity is hard and could cause friction. Pupils respond much more positively if you are honest with them and they can see you have their best interests at heart.

PLACING THE LEARNING CHALLENGE

Differentiation can mean a lot of different things. A traditional view is that materials are modified to meet the needs of the learner and make the learning accessible to them. This often results in words being substituted and content reduced for lower ability learners, white the most able get more lengthy and sophisticated accounts.

Now, consider the reverse.

USING COMPLEX WORDS WITH LOWER ABILITY PUPILS
We learn what objects or events are like through description. If the colour and vibrance is taken out of account, what is left for the memory to grab on to? Pupils respond much more to drama and excitement. A dramatic description of the flooding in Bangladesh could grip a Year 8 Geography class. Exploring alternative ways of describing the scene, or role-playing different words like 'manageable' or 'depressing' to find the most appropriate, would develop understanding.

WHERE SHOULD THE LEARNING CHALLENGE GO?
The question you choose for an assessment should not be altered for pupils of different abilities. What should change is where you ask pupils to make the leap forward. Effective learning and thinking happen when pupils are able to move just outside what they know, use new information and connect it to their existing knowledge. If we believe that pupils should be able to evaluate, then it should be explored by all.

A 'How important is . . . ?' question could be accessible to all, as long as sufficient background has been completed. Lower ability pupils might need time exploring the nature of the material, what is said and what can be seen; higher ability pupils might begin by examining what can be inferred from the information. Inference might be the middle stage in the progress of lower attainers and heavily supported, so that their learning challenge is putting together the evaluation.

Group work can be exciting and lead to some very innovative pupil work. Here are two ideas: one for managing mixed ability group work and one for differentiated groups.

ASSIGNING ROLES

Most extended group activities are going to require the pupils to perform a number of tasks. If you have put pupils in mixed-ability groups, then ensure you list a number of jobs and get pupils to sign up to them. For example, display work might contain the following roles:

O Researcher
O Photographer and imaging
O Writer
O Editor

When roles are clearly defined in this way, their talents can be matched to roles and everyone can to contribute effectively. You could even teach pupils about group dynamics and then get them to write down the skills they could offer, and allow groups to be formed in this way.

REPORTERS

If you wish to differentiate groups by ability, then you need to think about the kind of task each group will complete. Begin by designing questions of increasing complexity, but base them around a central focus or theme:

O What happened . . . ?
O Was . . . similar to . . . ?
O What factors lead to . . . ?
O Why is it difficult to . . . ?

This will enable each group to report back a significant part of the learning and feel like they are a part of the process. The most able can be reporters. It will be their job to visit each group and question the pupils. They must write a report for the class on how well each group worked and the importance of the work each group carried out. They can then begin the session by presenting their findings are so create links to move from one lesson to the next.

MANAGING DIFFERENTIATED GROUP WORK

Setting appropriate tasks for your pupils is crucial for their progression. Open-ended activities might work well for the more gifted in the class, but the less able require a more structured approach to learning. Exploring the learning styles of pupils in your class and then adapting your lessons accordingly will help challenge all pupils. Here are some activities that work for the various learning styles.

VISUAL LEARNERS: LEARN THROUGH SEEING

Pupils think in pictures and learn best from visual displays, including diagrams and illustrated textbooks, and tasks completed using flipcharts or Interactive Whiteboards. A variety of teaching methods would aid these learners, including concept mapping, laboratory experiments and story-boarding. More concrete activities are also useful, such as creating their own documentaries or editing ready-made footage to which they can add narration and text.

AUDITORY LEARNERS: LEARN THROUGH LISTENING

They learn most effectively through verbal instructions, discussions and debates. Asking them to conduct interviews, host panel discussions and undertake paired problem-solving are activities they most certainly will enjoy and learn from (See Idea 97 on starting a Podcast project – ideal for these learners!).

KINAESTHETIC LEARNERS: LEARN THROUGH A HANDS-ON APPROACH

These pupils learn most effectively through actively investigating the physical world around them. They may find it hard to concentrate while sitting down for longer periods, and can get distracted by their need for activity. Tasks such as Thinking Skills, categorization, matching tasks using physical objects, living diagrams and building or constructing things are activities these pupils love to undertake!

Finding the right balance for your pupils is crucial to help them learn. Providing activities for as many learning styles as possible will help your pupils progress further.

If you ever come across a pupil who is either very able or on your Gifted and Talented register, allow them to explore even the most elaborate of ideas. They will most likely do it well and the outcome of their learning will be staggering! If you decide to push these amazing individuals and are stuck for ideas, then try these and see if they enjoy them.

ENTERPRISE

This type of project has come popular recently, and is easy to set up either for younger or older pupils. Think of an idea such as a product or service that your pupils could potentially sell: perhaps a themed online journal that users subscribe to, or the construction of an ICT or language course that your pupil could teach primary school children.

There is ample funding available for Enterprise projects, as long as they have embedded the innovation in learning and teaching when the project is concluded. Enterprise projects can really enhance the whole school curriculum if planned well.

VIDEO EDITING

Suggest that pupils create an interactive project using, for instance, Windows Movie Maker or PowerPoint. They write a script or storyboard, record the footage they need and cut it into smaller chunks. Then they could for example create a map in PowerPoint with several hyperlinks added to it, so when a user clicks a particular area they are taken to a point in the presentation where one of these video clips are stored. Creating an investigation or a 'How to' guide are examples of what they could achieve with these tools.

These ideas are easily adapted for all subjects – imagination is everything! Your gifted pupils will find them exciting and they will also be pushed as far as it goes academically!

Enrichment tasks are activities that supplement the core curriculum and provide opportunities either to study subjects or content not covered in the general school timetable, or to conduct a more in-depth investigation of topics that are covered. The importance of enrichment is to allow pupils to respond innovatively and with imagination. Here are a few examples of activities that could be used.

MULTI-CULTURAL DAYS

Pupil groups cycle through a range of activities that explore and celebrate other cultures. Pupils could take crash courses in various languages, such as Greek, Hebrew or Egyptian hieroglyphs. Why not involve everyone in a big cooking session of Spanish paella or Japanese sushi?

THE THINK TANK

Pupils are given a number of problems to deal with or solve. Some of these could involve sorting and classifying information, predicting and testing hypotheses, or reasoning and evaluating solutions – that is, everything from mathematical problems to ethical dilemmas and issues concerning all of us such as the environment, racism or health and diet. The problems are intended to challenge pupils and extend their thinking. While some of them may be solved quickly (generally to warm them up!), others will need determination and may extend beyond an hour and span a series of lessons. The Think Tank challenges pupils to employ a range of skills to 'solve' these problems.

Enrichment is generally regarded as offering some of the best means of providing opportunities for potential to be released, as long as the activities are integrated within the curriculum rather than being an added extra. If it is organized in this manner, skills are easily transferred to other work.

Gifted and Talented pupils better to targets which are set collaboratively between the teacher and a small group of pupils. A project or assessment becomes more successful if the teacher can instruct them how to use a model for setting targets rather than getting involved in the process. A typical model for setting targets for a Gifted and Talented project could be as follows.

Pupils identify individual and group targets to move their work on. They are made aware of the end product and work they must complete, and then create a timetable. They produce short- and long-term work plans in order to drive themselves forward – they have to assess what should be done in each columns to make the end product realizable. At the end of each session pupils have to evaluate how far their skills have improved and to what extent they have met the targets they set. They then amend these for the next lesson to ensure they keep on track with the project. Here is a typical model that was used in a Year 9 Gifted and Talented history project, but which can easily be adapted for any subject.

Using target-setting and review provides pupils with a better focus for progression and forces them to address their learning needs. Consequently, each participant will have a clear idea of what their strengths and weaknesses are and will take these targets with them to the next scheme of work and assessment.

Example of Pupil Target Setting

Lesson 3		Lesson 4	
Group Target	**Individual Targets**	**Group Target**	**Individual Targets**
Formalize ideas about what to keep and what to change.	**Pupil 1** Investigate and decide on software for creating 3D model.	Create a 2D model of Dereham town centre 2020.	**Pupil 1** Begin work on the 3D model – create basic structure.
Begin to produce resources for presentation.	**Pupil 2** Draft an introduction for the presentation to establish principles of the project.	Begin virtual model.	**Pupil 2** Complete the introduction after consulting others about the draft.
	Pupil 3 Decide on PowerPoint template and begin to create presentation.		**Pupil 3** Work on PowerPoint and include ideas from others in the group.

Taken from Watkin and Ahrenfelt (2004)

Ensuring that your pupils have a sense of purpose to what they do is crucial, especially for Gifted and Talented pupils. They will respond much better if the activity they are undertaking actually leads to something concrete. The following activity provides them with a focus.

MAKE THEM MASTERS

Explain that after finishing a unit, pupils are to take part in a Master Class where they will be challenged on everything they have been taught. Set up the room as in the picture below. Divide the class into three groups and explain to them that they are to challenge each other's understanding. Therefore, they have to go through what they have studied and write down questions ranging from a scale from 1–20, where 1 is very easy and 20 very difficult. Team One will act as Panel Judges and sit along the row of tables, while Teams Two and Three will sit at one of the Team Tables. Each team chooses their first contestant and they sit facing the panel – The Master Class begins! Each contestant will receive 20 questions: if an answer is incorrect, the question goes to the opponent (therefore, it is possible to gain more than 20 points). After each team has sat in the chair and played the part as Panel Judges, the Master Class has finished and you can count the points.

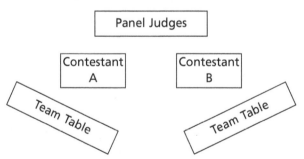

This exercise gives pupils a real outcome: but what did they achieve and what skills did they use? The preparation challenged them to work collaboratively as a group, they had to revise the content, and structure questions as well as think on their feet! Involving local businesses (such as museums) is also a good way of bringing real outcomes to Gifted and Talented work.

HAVE REAL OUTCOMES

73

Move Your Pupils On

DECIDE WHEN AND WHERE TO ASSESS

There is a need to assess pupils. As teachers, we must ensure that pupils are moving forward and progressing. We can plan for progression (see Idea 11), but it is important to know if pupils are keeping pace with our expectations.

Assessment should be used to move on pupil performance, and to inform planning. It needs to set up a cycle of learning so that pupils can review what has been achieved and then look towards improving their performance in the future.

The DfES identifies six purposes of assessment:

O Sharing learning objectives with pupils.
O Helping pupils to know and recognize the standards they are aiming for.
O Involving pupils in peer and self-assessment.
O Providing feedback that leads to recognizing their next steps and how to take them.
O Promoting confidence that every pupil can improve.
O Involving both teacher and pupil in reviewing and reflecting on assessment information.

The table opposite will help you make sense of assessment and where it will fit best.

When deciding when and where to assess,

DO NOT ...	INSTEAD ...
Use assessment too frequently.	Use an agreed mark scheme to assess three or four key pieces each year.
Assess only when asked to report on pupil attainment by senior managers.	Assess at regular intervals and make sure that each assessment supports pupil progression.
Assume that assessments need to come at the end of a unit.	Look at when pupils have completed significant work on a particular skill.
Opt for written tests every time.	Use a variety of assessments that have very different demands, such as oral presentations.
Try to assess everything at the same time.	Concentrate on a maximum of three skills (one of these could be literacy or numeracy).

SET CLEAR CRITERIA

It has long been common practice in schools to set clear objectives for a lesson. Objectives will help focus you and the pupils on what needs to be achieved and how it will be done. The phrase 'By the end of the lesson you will . . .' is now a permanent feature in classrooms.

If we apply the same principle to assessments, then we will get similar improvements. Having criteria will benefit everyone.

BENEFITS FOR PUPIL UNDERSTANDING

Clear criteria will help establish in the minds of pupils exactly what you are looking for. If they know you are going to assess three specific skills, then they know to concentrate on those elements of the work. Having the criteria means pupils can focus on what matters, rather than feeling their way through without knowing where they are really going.

BENEFITS FOR PUPIL ACHIEVEMENT

If you share the criteria with pupils, they can review their work as they go and perform accurate self-checking. They can focus on the work and what know how to achieve. This raises standards and motivation. It also avoids pupil disappointment at spending time on work and getting a low grade. If the criteria are shared you can work with them and suggest a redraft.

BENEFITS FOR MARKING

Having only three criteria to look for means you only need to identify where these have been met. Marking becomes more effective, because you will know individual strengths and weaknesses. It also has an impact on workload, because looking for where the criteria are met is more efficient: you focus on and mark what is important for pupil progression and greater understanding.

BENEFITS FOR PUPIL PROGRESS

Concentration on three areas helps pupils to make sense of work and to manage targets and steps for improvement.

Research into assessment and performance shows that when pupils see for themselves what they have to do in order to improve, they stand a better chance of reaching their targets. Build in opportunities for pupils to look critically at their work, and that of others.

REDRAFTING
Allowing pupils the chance to revisit work after it has been commented on is an effective way of tackling progression. The benefit of this is that pupils will gain a greater understanding of the success criteria and be able to work within them, seeing how they directly relate to the work they are doing.

If clear criteria have been set, then pupils could be involved in the whole process and peer-assess the first draft of the assignment. This will make pupils more aware of the demands of the piece and give them a chance to evaluate their own work in comparison to someone else's. Allowing them to engage with criteria at an early stage gives the process more coherence. Reviewing and redrafting can become normal parts of the creating process.

MARKING THE END PRODUCT
Pupils can also be involved in marking the final piece. This could be peer or self-assessment, as long as pupils explain their decision. Possibly, concentrate on one skill and get pupils to highlight in their work where it has been used.

TARGET-SETTING
Pupils will benefit from the setting of subject specific targets. If the criteria are precise and they have been given the opportunity to look at their work and that of others, they will be in a position to write something more meaningful than 'I will work harder next time'. Peer and self-assessment is about giving pupils the language to understand their own performance and comment on it. This approach is popular with pupils.

PEER AND SELF-ASSESSMENT

MEANINGFUL FEEDBACK

Once an assessment has been realized, it is time to get out the red pen and give the work a thorough marking. What you write is very important: the learning does not stop when the pupils finish the assessment, and your feedback could significantly move on the performance of pupils.

Feedback should have two basic features: point out and celebrate what pupils have done well, and show them how they can progress.

LOOKING AT THE POSITIVES IN PUPIL WORK

Praise is confidence-boosting. It will have greater impact if it is specific. Teachers often write 'Good work' or 'Excellent' in pupils' books, but what does it mean? What features have made it a good piece of work? If we want pupils to take note of the things they do well and make use of them again, we need to start using phrases that really explore what pupils have produced.

An alternative to writing a statement at the end is to highlight in each pupil's work where they have met the criteria. This is a very visual way of showing them how they achieved.

SETTING TARGETS

The purpose of the target is to look at a specific skill and suggest how the pupil can improve their work next time. Try to phrase this in positive language and concentrate on the possibilities. This could either be a statement or a question. Statements are easy to identify and apply to other pieces of work. Questions provide you with an opportunity to return immediately to the work with pupils and look at improvement. They can respond to your question and begin to see what that improvement should look like:

Statement: Back up your conclusions with evidence
Question: What evidence is there to back up your conclusion that . . . ?

Data can be an effective basis from which to start building a profile of the pupils that you teach (see Idea 77). However, you should also consider the following issues when looking at individual pupils and assessment.

USE LANGUAGE POSITIVELY

All pupils need to feel that they can achieve, and so assessment begins before the actual work starts. Show pupils that you have confidence in them and their ability to do well and be definite with your comments: 'I am certain you can do this.' Show that it is possible to achieve if problems are tackled in a positive way. This will lead to assured performances by pupils, and better quality assessment.

POTENTIAL VERSUS ACTUAL ACHIEVEMENT

Collect information about pupils that includes their actual test scores (such as SATs) and some measure of potential (like *MidYis*). This will enable you to see if the work they are producing is appropriate to their ability. If there is a discrepancy between the two, take action. Those achieving less than their potential can be given targets and monitored closely. Those out-performing their potential need to be given full recognition for their efforts and achievements.

KNOWING WHAT THEY WANT

Having a good grasp of the strengths and weaknesses of individual pupils helps to establish the right kind of tasks, and to give personalized feedback. Addressing pupil strengths and weaknesses is only possible if you know what they are. It is essential that assessment is used as a tool to build up a profile of the pupil, and this in turn becomes a way of setting targets for personal achievement. Dialogue between teacher and student is essential if this approach is to work.

KNOW YOUR PUPILS

Getting snowed under with marking has happened to all teachers at some point, and is not an experience any of us wish to relive. Follow these 'ticks' and you will find planning your marking just that little bit easier.

✓ Create a weekly timetable when you collect and return books – and stick to it.

✓ Start a 'Marking Club' with a bunch of teachers – biscuits provided by the weekly host. Getting that marking done with friends is a great way of easing the pressure!

✓ Use clever marking methods to cut down the amount you mark (see Idea 68).

✓ How can you make peer marking more effective?

✓ When marking is immense, treat yourself to a piece of chocolate for each book marked – speed tends to pick up for some reason . . .

✓ Make use of self-assessment and notice how the pupils improve!

✓ Read pupils' books in class: it not only gives you the opportunity to see how they are getting on in that lesson but it also keeps your marking down to a minimum.

✓ Use music while marking, as long as it is soft. Your favourite tunes might inspire you, but maybe not to mark!

✓ Whether the children are 11 or 18, they all love to receive stickers in their books and essays – get some personalized today!

A teacher's work is never done. Sometimes you need a break. Do not forget to try different methods so that you stay motivated!

There are many different approaches to marking and assessment, and some have been mentioned in this book. Trying to find ways to cut down marking is fairly easy, but have we thought about the purpose of marking children's book? How can we learn about our pupils and push them forward without disappearing under a mountain of books?

BE PROACTIVE

As often as possible, try going around the room reading pupils' work and commenting as you go along. For example, how often do children ask you to read or look at something? Here is an excellent opportunity to jot down a few comments, at the same time as you show an interest in their work.

CIRCLE TIME

Organize your room so that the chairs are in a circle with pupils facing each other. Choose a number of books and give the group a mark scheme (or an adapted one) to use. In pairs, ask them to read a piece of work, writing down three things they thought were good and two things they feel need improving, based on the mark scheme/criteria sheet. This method works well and the pupils find it rewarding to see others' work.

TARGET MARKING

Try marking one or two key pieces of work per group at Key Stage 3 per half term (if you are on a six-term timetable). The rest you simply go through and tick to check it is done and to make sure pupils know that you are aware and interested in their work – this saves time and frustration and prevents marking fatigue.

Keep this basic idea of marking in mind – you cannot mark each piece of work a pupil produces effectively, as you will never have time to plan or have a life. Therefore, don't do it.

You spend hours marking and writing valuable comments on pupils' work. Do pupils read your excellent suggestions or do they simply check the grade, ignoring the target advice? Which is more useful for pupil progression, grades or comments? After marking a few assessments, try to see if these handy methods make a difference.

STEP 1

Try not to write down a grade or level on their work. Instead, give detailed written feedback to pupils, and provide them with a verbal grade or level once they have taken the comments on board.

STEP 2

Set up a target sheet in your favourite word processing software and then print this off for pupils to stick into their books. They can then record their target relating from your feedback on the sheet. In this way their targets are easily accessible for both themselves as well as you the teacher. This method also makes report writing very straight forward!

STEP 3

After each major assessment, speak to a few pupils about their targets to see if they really understand what they need to do in order to progress further. Continue this over a few lessons until you have had a chance to speak to the whole class.

STEP 4

After a few weeks, or after a series of shorter assessments, discuss the issue of grades and levels with the class. Notice that most of them have stopped wondering about their grades and have begun thinking more about if, for example, they are using developed explanations rather than unsupported statements.

Using a combination of grades and detailed written or verbal feedback make pupils focus more on improving their work. Discussing their targets and asking why they received a certain grade instead of being content with their usual grade suddenly becomes more important.

Homework is an excellent tool for extending pupils' thinking, but it tends to focus more on writing, which can get monotonous for pupils and add an extra marking load for you.

DESCRIBE IT!

Give each pupil an image to describe to an adult, for example a parent or guardian, and then have their books signed for you to check in the next lesson.

EXPLAIN IT!

Ask pupils to explain one aspect of the lesson to another person outside of school. When they come back to your lesson, their explanations will also be great as starters to recap the previous lesson!

CRITICIZE IT!

Give each pupil a quote or image to scrutinize, based around a set of criteria that you also give them. Next lesson ask them to inform the person sitting next to them about what they discovered. If planned carefully, this homework could lead into this lesson.

Setting non-written homework not only improves pupils' communication skills and boosts their self-esteem, but also helps reduce your mark load. Other tasks could focus on, for example, taking a concept further, exploring an idea more broadly, interpreting the same task differently or learning an additional concept.

USE HOMEWORK TO ENHANCE COMMUNICATION SKILLS

CONSOLIDATE THEIR LEARNING

STARTERS

Create beginnings that look at what you focused on in the previous lesson. For example, write down key words on 20 or so Post-it notes and place them on walls around the room. Then ask pupils to grab one and explain it to the rest of the class.

OVERVIEWS AND LINKS

Ask the class how the last lesson links in with the current one: if that is difficult, maybe they can find common themes or factors between the two. Then see if they can do the same thing with the previous unit or module. This is generally very challenging for most classes, but with a bit of scaffolding it can be done, even if lessons seem to share very few common features. Record their findings so that it becomes easier for them to see the links.

PLENARIES

This plenary can easily be linked in with the starter described above. While the pupils work, write down a few new concepts or key words learnt in this lesson on Post-it notes. Ask for a volunteer and explain that they are to act out (like charades) the content of the Post-it without speaking. The class tries to guess (or giggles!) their way to the correct answer.

HOMEWORK

Reinforce knowledge gained in the lesson by setting them homework that extends their learning. For example, ask them to summarize the lesson in 30 words or fewer, or to explain the purpose of the lesson or unit and why they need to study it.

'Extension' is the method of providing stimulation and more challenge, rather than 'follow-up work' which generally means to do more of the same. The latter is likely to demotivate pupils and therefore have an adverse effect on their learning.

THE MESSENGER

Split the class into groups of three or four and tell them that they are to find out about a particular topic within a certain time, and they have to explain their findings to each other without speaking. Ask them to use Microsoft Messenger to communicate with the rest of the group. This is a fantastic tool for practising thinking on their feet and writing coherently so that their team members understand. A good idea could be to set a competitive element to this, with the whole class trying to find out information about a particular subject and the first one to solve the problem crowned as the winner.

THE 'LINK' EFFECT

This activity may be best suited for the more able groups. Split the class into groups of two or three and inform them that they are to find a number of web links that relate to the lesson. They need to drag these into a folder so that others can access them later. The group then needs to think of questions about the current topic that the rest of the class can find the answers to in the web links. To spice things up a bit, inform them that they should also be able to point out where in the site answers can be found. This ensures that they choose links that are suitable for the class.

These extension activities focus on taking pupil learning to the next level, while at the same time improving their literacy and ICT skills. They can be adapted to suit any subject and, if planned carefully, any class.

EXTEND THEIR LEARNING

Good teachers always find ways to explain how each element of their teaching links together, so that pupils know that the current lesson will provide them with knowledge and understanding that will enable them to deal with the challenges of the next one.

POSTERS

One way of making pupils feel more in control of their own learning is to place a pupil copy of your schemes of work by the door, so they can take a quick look to see what they are doing in the various lessons.

HOMEWORK

Homework is an effective way to prepare pupils for the next lesson. For example, setting research tasks encourages them to read independently, as they might be challenged by a fellow pupil if they have not done enough reading.

FAMOUS LAST WORDS

The very end of the lesson when the class is waiting patiently behind their chairs is a good opportunity to explain to them what they will be doing over the next few lessons. Telling pupils why these lessons follow on from each other can also be valuable, as it provides an overview that can easily be discussed further at a later date when they are ready.

Explaining to the class what the next lesson will entail is good practice as it assists the children to gain a sense of purpose and it also helps to consolidate their learning much more effectively.

Getting pupils to respond to your comments helps you to
see if they have understood and gives them the
opportunity to be critical of their own learning.

WHY NOT . . .

O Make comments a little more personal by using their
names in your comments.
O Encourage pupils to get into dialogue with you by
asking them to write down an answer to your
comments.
O Provide more extensive analytical feedback less
regularly (for example, once a half term) if lack of
time is factor.

THE DIALOGUE

At the start of each lesson, ask pupils to respond to your
comments. Then during the next few lessons ask them to
bring their book to your desk to see what they have
written and why. If they have not responded, then you
could always ask them to do it again while they are there:
chances are that they did not understand what you
wanted them do. This also gives you an opportunity to
speak to them individually about how they are getting on.

PEER MARKING

When pupils mark each other's work they tend to
respond well to targets set by them and to positive
comments. Allowing them to think about what
comments and targets to write also makes them aware of
your role as a teachers and gives them the opportunity to
see how well other people work.

Keeping up a running dialogue, either verbal or written,
is an effective way to communicate with your class and it
also makes them aware of their own progression.

GET PUPILS TO RESPOND TO FEEDBACK

NEXT STEPS APPROACH

This is heavily linked to feedback (see Idea 64), but deserves a separate mention if only to focus attention on it as an important part in the assessment process. Once dialogue on the assessment has taken place, targets need to be set.

TARGETS

The point of a target is to show pupils where they can go next to improve their work. It should be achievable and linked to the work they have just completed. In other words, the target represents the 'next step' pupils should take in mastering a particular skill. It gives pupils something to work towards.

This process is still only half complete. Both teacher *and* pupils need to consider what the next steps will be and how to put them into practice.

PUPILS AND NEXT STEPS

Pupils should come out of the assignment with one target, or possibly two. They need to reflect on these targets and do something with them. They will need some quick reference points when using them, and possibly a way of organizing them.

TEACHERS AND NEXT STEPS

Teachers have helped to set the targets and so they need to ensure that opportunity is given to pupils to revisit that skill (or skills) and put their plan into action. The targets will only be meaningful if pupils act upon them.

If you are setting clear objectives for the lesson and these are driven by the skills inherent in your subject, pupils should have no trouble identifying which pieces of work apply to their targets. You could even have a target review session every so often, in which you ask pupils to look at the work they have done since receiving their target and to record any progress they have made.

Keeping clear records is an important part of the job. If your school has a clear homework policy then you have to ensure that pupils stick to it. This means formally recording who has handed in work and who has not.

Traditionally, teachers use their mark book to record grades and test scores. As an alternative, note down the targets pupils were set after completing an assessment. Track their progress and write down the date on which they completed them. Then, record their new target in your mark book.

This will give you a wealth of meaningful information about each student. When it comes to writing their school report, you will have plenty to say regarding strengths and weaknesses and the rate of their progress. At parents' evening, you can have an informed discussion with parents about the areas of learning in which they can offer support, rather than having to say, 'Well, she has got a couple of Ds this year, but the rest of her work has been C grade standard.'

If you do need to report on levels, take a look at your National Curriculum level descriptors and decide which one best fits the performance of the pupil. This is how they are intended to be used anyway.

RECORD-KEEPING AND ORGANIZATION

DEALING WITH PUPIL PROGRESSION

The idea of progression is not a new one, but planning for it might be (see Ideas 11 and 61). When pupils have completed an assessment and revisited targets, they will have made some progress. What remains for the teacher to do is to ensure that it is not an isolated incident, but part of a structured and coherent programme designed to maximize learning.

WHERE TO START

Go back to your progression charts and look at what skills you feel are important to develop with each year group. Have these in front of you as you work on the next exercise.

Decide what it is that you want pupils to achieve by the end of each year. This can be done by constructing a simple table. Look at what you teach in each term (at this stage, keep to broad headings) and jot down what skills you wish to develop with pupils and how far you want them to get. Make sure that each new unit builds on the last. It is important to revisit skills and concepts, but ensure that a level of complexity is added so that progress is planned.

If you want to look at differentiation, then you could decide what 'all pupils', 'most pupils', 'some pupils' will achieve by the end of each unit. 'All pupils' represents a basic progression, 'most' is what you see as an average and 'some' marks the level expected of higher achieving pupils.

Extend this work across an entire Key Stage. This will enable you to see exactly what progression pupils would or could make over a number of years. Having this overview will allow you to better advise pupils of their next steps and monitor their effectiveness. In essence, you will be creating your own taxonomy of learning.

Working With Your Pupils

USING DATA EFFECTIVELY

Teachers are swimming in data, and yet it is rarely used because staff make their own judgements about the progression of pupils. Teacher input and assessment is vital for building a picture of what a pupil is achieving. Therefore, teachers should collect data from assessed pieces and use it to inform their planning. For example, a History assessment about Native American culture might look at the issue of cause and consequence. Once the assessment is complete, the teacher can look at the data and make decisions about subsequent lessons. If most of the class have completed the assessment to a high standard then the teacher can move on with the skill, and design lessons that consider events with multiple consequences. However, if the class have struggled the teacher can instantly see that the skill will need revisiting and the core concepts reinforced before the class moves on.

Establishing your own data is a valuable way to make meaning link to the work you are doing with pupils. Trying to describe the extent worth of a National Curriculum Level 6 to pupils is not easy, but working with them to increase their understanding of a specific skill or concept is realizable.

Self-generated data is less effective at recognizing potential. Some pupils may disguise their true talents, or possibly have not discovered the right methods needed to unlock them. Outside data that looks at potential should be used as a way to inform you and pupils of the standard you wish to see. It is not a stick with which to beat pupils, but a way of recognizing that someone may not be progressing at a rate that is equal to their abilities.

Establishing the right kind of relationship can be helped by focusing on the areas below.

SET EFFECTIVE RULES

Start the year by negotiating and setting rules with the aid of pupil input: successful teachers are clear about what will be acceptable. Investing time on rules before teaching begins is a good way to establish positive behaviour.

BUILD ROUTINES

It is important for learners to feel safe and be treated fairly. For this to happen, routines need to be established and used rigidly. An orderly start is important, and if the teacher can be already in the room before the pupils a clear message is sent out that once they enter the learning will begin. The same principle applies to the end of a lesson, where pupils should leave in an orderly way. Have a clear pattern to your lesson (such as always using starters/plenaries). Let pupils know that homework is of value: make sure that it is set regularly. Chase up those who fail to bring in work and have sanctions in place.

Also, consider the following:

THE ACADEMIC

Knowing what drives pupils forward is crucial to their continued development. Are they on target or do they seem to coast their way through lessons? There may be some that have been targeted for various reasons, for example Gifted and Talented pupils.

THE SOCIAL

Some challenging pupils respond well to praise. Are there issues outside school that affect their behaviour in class? There may also be medical information about pupils that would be worth knowing, in case of an emergency.

Knowing interesting facts about pupils (such as if they do sports, what music they like, etc.) helps to foster professional relationships in which they understand that we are genuinely interested in them as human beings as well as pupils.

BUILDING THE RIGHT KIND OF RELATIONSHIPS

PUPIL QUESTIONNAIRES

The high street works on a diet of consumer surveys and customer relations. The establishment of a pupil voice can be a starting point for establishing an exciting and self-motivating experience in your class room.

When you have completed a section of work, simply give out a sheet that asks pupils to list their favourite and least enjoyable parts of the unit. Ask them if anything was difficult, or too easy. Question them about what they found useful and what they feel they have achieved. An interesting way to end is to ask how they would have structured the learning sequence. This last activity is a great way to end Key Stage 3: give pupils an overview and a selection of textbooks and get them to establish the content of the 11–14 curriculum.

You could take this a step further. If you feel brave enough, ask pupils to evaluate your teaching. Pupils can use a numbered scale to rate the various parts of the lesson (starters, objectives, homework, etc.), the atmosphere in the class, their level of understanding and sense of achievement. You could even ask pupils to shade in the components they think are most vital for a successful lesson and compare that to where they have given you high scores.

Working with pupils in this manner will give you a valuable insight into how you come across in the classroom. It will also make pupils feel like their voice matters, and they will be more inclined to cooperate in future activities if they know their opinion counts.

You could also devise questionnaires to explore their likes and dislikes about your subject, or get them to fill in a learning styles questionnaire, so that you can see if the class has a strong preference for a particular way of learning.

Sometimes you have frustrating lessons, in which good planning and execution go to waste due to disinterested students, or a negative response. If this is happening, then it might be worth looking at the learning environment to see if it can be improved in order to stimulate that interest.

Your teaching room needs to send out the message that is a place for learning. It should therefore be centred around learning and aim to assist in it. A stimulating classroom will provide pupils with all the information they need to succeed.

DISPLAYING PUPIL WORK

Displaying work acts as a motivator. Pupils know that you take pride in their work, and it sets expectations about the level of response you require. First, try to place work just above eye level, where it can be noticed and accessed easily. Ensure that the work displayed is of good quality – otherwise the value is diminished, in the eyes of pupils. When you have work worth showing, it is worth showing well, so frame it with strong colours and, if possible, use a laminator. In addition, create small labels to point out interesting parts, or where a skill has been well demonstrated – this means it can be used as a teaching aid.

PROMOTING SKILLS

Displays do not only have to be of pupil work. Have a board that looks at key skills in your subject, or supports literacy and genre. This type of display should be related to the teaching currently going on and referred to on a regular basis by the teacher. It can become a valuable tool in the classroom and be used independently by pupils as a way of checking their own learning. Change all displays regularly.

Pupils like the thought of group work, and it engages them with an activity. Designing a lesson that has collaborative elements is fairly easy, but it is more difficult to manage group work so that pupils are working effectively and developing their skills of interaction and cooperation. Yet employers are searching for people who can work as part of a team and are able to fit into an existing organization.

DEVELOP TEAM WORK

Allow pupils to choose their own groups for a good proportion of activities: this is an easy way to make them feel comfortable and motivated. Every so often, get them to work with new people. Explain the possible benefits of this and then evaluate the experience at the end of the task.

INCREASING INTERACTION

A clever way of increasing participation is to build up to a group response. Start individually or in pairs, and once everyone has thought of a series of points move into bigger groups. Once in groups, interaction can be improved by having a lengthy planning stage. Insist that pupils have a minimum of 15 ideas before deciding on a final course of action.

BUILDING COOPERATION

Assigning roles and responsibilities is an effective way to ensure that all pupils are involved. Beyond this, get groups to set themselves mini-targets to achieve, and review them on a regular basis.

NEGOTIATION SKILLS

There are two strategies here. First, use a range of problem-solving activities in class. Second, get pupils to evaluate how the group worked and outline the problems they encountered. Ask them to say how they would have solved these problems. Complete a similar task within a reasonable time and ask each group to focus on these improvements.

Drama teachers hate Year 9 options evening: a long line of parents will ask the question, 'How's drama going to help them get a job then?' Of all the key skills that exist in schools, communication is the one we use the most – but it is the one pupils will need to develop and be successful at deploying if they want to succeed in life.

Communication skills should to be a focus for every subject and explored in all its forms. Written communication is used all the time, but the idea can be extended to incorporate different genres of writing and to give pupils a sense of audience. This does not have to become a straight literacy exercise with no bearing on the core curriculum. For example, a Technology lesson might focus on the production of page for a DIY manual, or presenting design ideas to a room of potential clients. There could be scope to look at marketing and to get the class to run a stall at a mock-trade fair once they have designed and realized a product.

Verbal communication is vital. Allowing pupils the opportunity to discuss ideas and work out problems is an essential part of learning. Group work generates enthusiasm and interest, as well as good quality work. When developed correctly, it teaches pupils about deadlines, cooperation and roles and responsibilities. In order for this to happen successfully, you should:

O Establish class rules for group work.
O Have clear objectives and timescales.
O Get pupils to assign themselves roles.
O Encourage pupils to set mini targets.

The words 'communication skills' should feature regularly in the objectives of lessons. It should be the aim of all teachers to make their pupils confident and able communicators, who know how to adapt content to fit audience and genre.

COMMUNICATION – THE FORGOTTEN SKILL!

REASONING AND JUDGEMENT

Teachers have a duty to equip pupils for the world they will face when they leave school. At present, this is a planet full of media and technology. Information hits them at a rapid rate and it can be found continuously. It could be argued that pupils will face too much information and therefore, it is up to the teacher to help them cope with this situation.

There is now little beyond the reach of individuals: whatever they need to know is 'out there'. However, content is not well-regulated and so the skills of reasoning and judgement have become more important than ever. Try these ideas:

SHOWING PUPILS HOW THE INTERNET WORKS

Allan November tells a great story:

The following story is also true.

Fourteen year old: 'I'm working on a history paper about how the Holocaust never happened.'

Long pause. 'Zack, where did you hear that the Holocaust didn't happen?'

'The Internet. It's on a Web page at Northwestern University.'

Zack found his 'information' from a Web page at http://pubweb.acns.nwu.edu/~abutz/index.html, titled 'Home Web page of Arthur R. Butz.' On his low-key home page, Butz explains that he wrote 'A short introduction to the study of Holocaust revisionism' and that his material is intended for 'advanced students of Holocaust revisionism.' At the top of the page Butz identifies himself as 'Associate Professor of Electrical and Computer Engineering, Northwestern University.'

(Allan November, Teaching Zack to Think)

This demonstrates to pupils the dangers of using the internet without reading the content carefully and cross-referencing what is said. Incidentally, the views above were expressed on a personal page (indicated by the '~' symbol).

DECONSTRUCTING ADVERTS

Using your subject content as a basis, get pupils to advertise a product effectively. Analyse how adverts persuade before you start.

Consider for a minute the weekly life of a pupil. They will probably study some 13 subjects, with as many different teachers. That means 13 styles of presentation and 13 separate agendas. They will experience little support to make sense of all this. However, research has clearly indicated that the most effective learners are the ones who can make connections and successfully categorize their new learning. As class teachers, we have a large role to play in working with pupils to make this happen.

NUMERACY AND LITERACY

There have been national attempts to achieve joined-up learning in this area with the Literacy and Numeracy strategies. Covering elements of this within your lessons is an excellent way of helping pupils to join up their learning. Collating data is going to be the same in Maths as it is in Geography, and having the word 'numeracy skills' in your objectives will help pupils to recognize that learning is transferable.

JOINED-UP PLENARIES

Some skills are universal, like problem-solving, categorization, or using and improving memory. If you cover one of these within a lesson, then leave a little extra time in your plenary to explore the links to other subjects. Only by being asked to think about the wider use of a skill will pupils become used to transferring their skills and using them in different situations.

PROGRESSION SCHEMES

Take another look at Idea 12 on 'Bloom's Taxonomy'. If a number of teachers agree to use a system like this then pupils will be able to make sense of their own progression. Even if you are going it alone with Bloom's Taxonomy, there are clear benefits. You can pull out the stages that are applicable to any subject and draw these out in your joined-up plenaries.

START WITH THE FAMILIAR

The challenge for the teacher is to engage pupils with an activity involving new concepts without taking them out of their depth. There is an easy way of doing this: start with something familiar to the pupils and then build the lesson from there, moving slowly to the unfamiliar and allowing pupils to draw on what they know and to connect the new material to it. This foundation can be achieved in one of two ways.

THE RECAP

There are a number of exciting ways to recap on the previous lesson (see Ideas 13 and 34 for good examples), and homework can be used in the same way. Set a task that builds on the knowledge of the lesson and then make it the focus of your starter. For example, any piece of work that involves persuasive writing can be turned into a mini contest. Get four volunteers and have them stand at compass points in the room. They can then use their homework content to persuade the other members of the group to join them. The class listen to all four arguments and then choose a person to stand by. Question pupils about their choice and the reasons for it. If you can squeeze in extra rounds and allow pupils to change their mind then it becomes even more valuable as an exercise.

CONCRETE EXAMPLES FOR ABSTRACT CONCEPTS

When introducing a new idea that is mostly theoretical (such as power, ownership or sustainability) begin the lesson with a familiar example. The idea of 'fairness' might be introduced by the pupils rewriting the rewards and sanctions policies within school. Or they might take a recent news event or court case and express their opinion about the results: 'Should fox hunting be allowed?', for example. Any issue is valid, so long as pupils have an opinion.

It can be quite difficult to hook pupils into an activity and link it to their lives. One way of achieving this is to use current personalities to help present the work.

ANALOGY

There is a lot of information about celebrities and their lives. It will not be difficult to find a pattern in the behaviour of one of them that matches the topic you are about to teach. If you can phrase this as a question it will have even more impact: 'Why is Alex Ferguson similar to . . . ?'

PRESENTER

Another option is to get a personality to present the lesson. Simply find an image of your chosen star and add a speech bubble. This increases engagement with the material and adds an element of fun. If you need to show differing opinions, find two celebrities at war and get them to argue the points (in speech bubbles). Begin with '[A] and [B] are always disagreeing. First it was [famous argument] and now it is [your topic].'

CELEBRITY CONCEPTS

If there is a concept you need to explain, TV celebrities can make it accessible. For example, work that involves linking and patterns can be introduced by the family tree of a soap family (there is always someone who has secret love child, and so the links are complex).

SOAP REWRITES

Soap operas offer many opportunities to check understanding. They can be rewritten to have a different central theme or issue (terrorism), or the setting can be changed to look at 'place' (*EastEnders* set in Kenya). They can be moved to another time period (Tudor *Coronation Street*), or spoken in another language. The idea is to check whether pupils have grasped the topic being studied, and working in this way adds a level of complexity alongside a level of familiarity.

Pupils experience a world of instantaneous and interactive media. It is fast-paced and exciting. If we want to capture their imagination then we must use the kind of tools that they know and use.

VIDEO CLIPS

Resist the temptation to show lengthy videos that take up an entire lesson: a short clip of 5 to 15 minutes can be just as effective. By using cheap software and possibly some hardware you can create digital footage and use it on the interactive whiteboard. If you have a longer video that is vital to the topic being studied, then try targeted viewing. If there are four areas you wish pupils to focus on, then put them in teams of four and assign one area to each pupil. This makes observation more manageable for pupils and will naturally lead into a communication task straight afterwards.

COMPUTERS

This field in constantly changing, but as a general rule avoid straight copying or repetition. The internet is fantastic and there are many resources that can be used, but they must be just that: 'used'. Too many pupils copy and paste without reading or synthesizing; activities must take this into account, maybe by setting word limits or giving pupils specific links to look at. Creating your own image bank will discourage time-wasting and bring the focus back to the content and skills. Applications that automatically encourage selection and manipulation, such as Moviemaker, can be really valuable. PowerPoint is also useful, but be strict with the number of slides and even the number of words per slide.

Pupils know best what technology motivates them – I have recently seen a mobile phone alarm clock used to create a light and sound show! Engaging pupils in this way will encourage them to work with you.

Pupils are more engaged and ready to respond when they are comfortable with the subject material. If they have had direct experience of the matter, then discussion is even livelier. If teachers are working with pupils and trying to motivate them, there is no better way than making lessons relevant to their lives – and this need not be a major undertaking.

STARTER

Before beginning a problem-solving lesson, ask pupils to name some TV detectives and then outline the work they do. Explain that they will be using the same techniques in the lesson, in order to solve a problem.

LESSON IDEA

Establish a point of interest outside school and exploit this, or use a family connection to structure the lesson. For example, use the format of a pop song to write a summary of the topic or unit studied. Alternatively, a Food Technology lesson about altering recipes could start by pupils picking an ingredient that someone in their house does not like. They would then find a recipe that contains this and adapt it.

PLENARY

When you have developed a skill within a lesson and discussed what you have learned and how, finish by asking pupils where that skill could be used outside school. This could be done by breaking it down into careers and jobs, or situations. You might even get them to think back over the past few days and identify something they could have done better if they had used that particular skill.

The experiences of pupils outside of school are very important to them. If you bring their families, locality and cultural background into the classroom, they are more likely to engage with the learning.

Bring Order to Your Teaching Life

GRAB THEIR ATTENTION

It can be difficult to walk into a class you have never taught before, especially if the pupils are quite noisy. What can we do as teachers not only to grab their attention but also to maintain it?

MAKE YOURSELF KNOWN

Try using signals and tools, such as knocking on the desk or simply announcing that you would like to start the lesson. This makes pupils realize that you are not only in the classroom, but you are ready to teach them.

RESPECT THEM

Walking into a class shouting and screaming, even if they do not quiet down instantly, only makes them resent you, and their behaviour will probably deteriorate later on even if they settle down initially.

'HOOK' THEM

The good old fashion hook generally grabs their attention! Try drawing something which would be out of character for a teacher, like graffiti, or attempt to draw a picture of something that you are to discuss in the lesson – the worse you are as an artist the better! (see Section 4 for other ideas about 'hooks'.)

INSPIRE THEM

How could you use the pupils themselves in the lesson from the start? Have they got something with them that you could use as an example of what you teach? Using a simple quote, outrageous statistic, website or Podcast (see Idea 97) can also help focus their attention.

Grabbing a class's attention is all about reaching the pupils in some way. There are teachers that are able to walk into a classroom and have the pupils mesmerized from the onset. They have managed to connect with their classes. Perhaps the best way to get pupils focused is through making them see that your lessons are simply too good to miss out on!

Making sure that pupils get on task and, most importantly, stay on task, requires teachers to challenge them and push them into wanting to learn. Bear these short tips in mind next time you are planning a lesson.

KEEP IT SNAPPY

Ensure that you plan a few short, sharp and focused activities that naturally lead into each other. Keep the pace between tasks and make sure that your transitions are tight (see Section 3 for ideas on pace and transitions).

INVOLVE THEM

Encourage pupils to do things which you would normally have to do. For instance, have pupils creating mind maps on the board during whole-class discussions, or handing out books or other resources. This allows you to face the class more in order to encourage your pupils to work.

VARIATION IS GOLDEN

Check through your lesson plans to see what type of activities you use in your lessons. How often are you talking to them or using PowerPoint presentations, for example? Try using tasks that challenge different learning styles in each lesson by using music, images, text or digital video.

LET THEM TEACH

Depending on the class, asking them to teach part of a lesson can work wonders as they get a quick glance at what you do before every lesson! Teach them the ground rules of a good lesson, even about aim and objectives – you will be surprised how much they actually know about teaching!

These ideas work very well when planned carefully, particularly the last one. Even if it does not work the first time, the pupils will enjoy what they have done and learning will take place anyway. Try planning a lesson with only short quick activities and see what result you get.

Sometimes children do not seem to be able to listen to what you have to say. Try these hints and see if they help.

STEP 1

Ask yourself if there are several classes that struggle to pay attention, or is it only one or two? If there are more than two then it would be a good idea to have someone observe a couple of lessons and give you feedback. If there is only one or two, then chances are that it is a mixture of issues such as time of day, where pupils are sitting and your own planning.

STEP 2

Have you included too much of one element? Make sure that you have integrated tasks to suit all abilities and learning styles (this cannot happen in a single lesson as it would be impossible to cater for everyone, but is possible over a series of lessons). Check carefully what type of tasks you are planning: for example, what proportion of the lesson do you spend talking, including instructions and taking the register?

STEP 3

Also, check the timings of tasks: how you ensure that pace is maintained and that transitions are used effectively to ensure a smooth-running lesson (see Section 3 for ideas)?

STEP 4

Make use of expert help and the colleagues around you. There will be someone in school who has responsibility for planning and ensuring continued professional development of staff. Ask them to observe your teaching informally and offer advice on how to tackle the issue. Alternatively, get in touch with an advanced skills teacher whom you can work alongside. If possible, do an exchange and observe each other teach.

These steps have focused on the practitioners themselves rather than the pupils. Checking lesson plans is generally a good way of finding out what the problems might be.

On average, pupils need two seconds of 'thinking time' to be able to answer a question – teachers give pupils about one second to respond to a question. If we are to aid pupils' cognitive development, we need to give them a chance to think, otherwise they will not learn or understand.

TIP 1

After asking the question, count to ten and then choose someone to speak.

TIP 2

Have ready-made pupil name cards, which you laminate so you can re-use them over and over again. Place these cards in a bag or hat, etc., and each time you ask a question pick a name out of the bag and let that pupil answer the query.

TIP 3

Inform one section of the room, for example the row nearest to the window, that you will ask them a question about a certain issue in three minutes. In the meantime, ask other members of the class.

TIP 4

Do not forget to ask lower order cognitive questions such as recollection and comprehension, as well as higher order questions such as analysis and evaluation.

TIP 5

For immediate response and to check what proportion of the class has understood, why not use mini whiteboards (see Section 2)?

The way teachers check understanding varies from practitioner to practitioner and depending on the class being taught. Thinking of their development within the lesson is also important and these easily adaptable tips will hopefully assist you.

WHY DON'T THEY UNDERSTAND?

OBSERVE SPECIALISTS

Whether you are new to the teaching profession or an old hand, it is useful to compare the way you teach with other practitioners. Here are a few ideas what to look out for in a good lesson.

QUESTIONING

There are teachers who manage to include the whole class in every lesson – how do they do it? Note down what type of questioning they are using, where in the room the teacher is scanning for hands up, and how they adapt their questions. Remember the time it takes for pupils to think (see Idea 92): how is this teacher dealing with it?

BEHAVIOUR

Some teachers stand out from the rest when it comes to classroom management. Note the way teachers speak to the class. It may come naturally to them, but you can adopt strategies to achieve the same thing.

GIFTED AND TALENTED

Most schools have someone in charge of their Gifted and Talented policy. How do they extend these able pupils' learning? What methods do they use? Pay particular attention to the way the lesson is structured: you may notice that it is fairly open-ended for some of the pupils and more structured for others.

ADVANCED SKILLS TEACHERS

If you are lucky, your school will have employed one. Otherwise, check with your local county council and they will be able to assist you. Phone up and ask if you could observe them and make sure that you specify what you would like to look at if possible. Note that many advanced skills teachers have certain specialisms.

Targeted observations of excellent classroom practitioners who have certain strengths is a valuable tool if you wish to develop as a teacher. Make sure that you ask colleagues about teachers in your school who they have observed and found inspiring.

Ever felt like someone is watching you? If the answer is no, then ask a colleague to film one of your lessons. It is amazing what you learn about yourself as a classroom practitioner after watching only one lesson.

THE WAY YOU SPEAK

If you notice that you keep using the same words or noises such as 'yeah', 'excellent', or 'hmm . . .' and you find that irritating, then imagine what it must be like hearing this for three hours a week!

Notice how often and in what way you use praise. Are you using praise such as 'Good girl!' or 'Well done!' or more personal praise, for example 'I like the way you have explained . . .', or 'What a good idea to . . .'.

THE WAY YOU MOVE

Are you an anchor or goal keeper? That is, do you stay in the same place or do you run side to side for an hour? Are there areas of the classroom that you tend to spend longer in than others?

THE WAY YOU INTERACT

Notice how your body language changes throughout the lesson and how pupils respond to you. Some teachers change the way they teach quite drastically depending on the class. If you film a series of lessons with various year groups and abilities, you soon realize that your style of teaching vary slightly. Perhaps one way of teaching a particular class could also work wonders with another? Also, try to recognize if you scan the room before taking an answer – how long do you give them?

Being filmed by a colleague really can work wonders with your professional development and it gives you a good indication of why things are going well, or why they are not. Watching yourself in action is, on top of everything else, fun!

Teaching should be about exploration, implementation and reflection. It is when these aspects blend together that the teacher has the opportunity to experience real progression. Let us not forget why we, the educators, are here and what the purpose of teaching actually is: to train a new generation of children to become mature, level-headed individuals, professionals who will eventually lead our companies, run our country and most crucially teach our children and take care of us when we grow older.

If we can accept our purpose in the world of learners, then how can we ensure that this new generation is successful? Children can lose touch with education and quickly forget the point of it all. If we do not remind them then we have failed them. Should we not stimulate young children into becoming critical learners, who are confident and independent – engaged learners, who can gain a sense of ownership of the taught knowledge? If we can achieve that, then we have succeeded.

Learning is a human right. It is a need that is inherent in us as humans and it is articulated in various ways throughout the history of all people. Let us ensure that we provide a challenging and enriching experience for our learners so that they can look back and say their education was the cornerstone of who they have become as individuals.

Regard the classroom as a kind of laboratory where you, the teacher, can relate teaching theory to teaching practice. Excellent classroom practitioners constantly strive to think of new ways to progress, both in terms of subject knowledge and professional strategies. Think about these things and see if they give you some new ideas.

WHAT WENT WELL?

If you just focus on your own teaching, you may never create that 'perfect lesson'. Ask those who have experience of your teaching – the pupils. In one lesson ask a few pupils from various abilities about the lesson that you delivered. Write down their comments. Then ask the same pupils to do it again, but this time give them a sheet of questions to answer: Did you understand the aims and objectives of the lesson? What did you enjoy about this lesson? Letting them watch more than once enables the pupils to become good at lesson observations. After the final observation, discuss their answers.

HOW WELL IS IT WORKING?

If you look at pupil learning as a measurement of your teaching skills, then you quickly realize how far your methods work. How effective were you?

HOW CAN I IMPROVE AS AN EDUCATOR?

Use the information received from your pupils' observations and really think about what you can do, not only to challenge them and make them learn, but also so that it is interesting for them.

Trying new teaching strategies is the key to becoming a great reflective practitioner. We need to examine our beliefs and philosophy about education and integrate these into our teaching. Constantly striving forward is the main tool we have as educators to ensure that we do not grow roots and stagnate.

A REFLECTIVE PRACTITIONER'S ACTION PLAN

START A TEACHING AND LEARNING PROJECT

Stay ahead and take control over your own professional development by starting an innovative project that you can share with your school, department and colleagues. Here is an example of what you could do: 'Podcasting'.

WHAT IS 'PODCASTING'?

A 'Podcast' is a web feed of audio or video files placed on the internet for anyone to subscribe to. They could also be downloaded directly from Podcasters' websites, but the subscription feed of automatically delivered new content is what differentiates a Podcast from a straightforward download.

WHAT DEVICE DO I NEED TO LISTEN TO PODCASTS?

Although the term 'Podcasting' mainly refers to the iPod because many use it to listen to Podcasts, subscribing to a Podcast does not mean you have to play it on an Apple-made gadget. There are literally thousands of tools available to receive them and you can use either your computer or MP3 player to play them. Podcasting is just the way they are delivered.

WHY SHOULD TEACHERS GET INVOLVED WITH PODCASTING?

Teachers always try new methods to reach children and get them inspired to learn and, most importantly, to take charge of their own learning. Tapping into a resource that enables you to create lessons, revision content, documentaries and state-of-the-art homework (oh yes!) that is available for pupils to listen or watch wherever they are can only be a good thing. Imagine creating homework which the pupils can listen to on their MP3 players and get updates on as soon as it becomes available.

Starting innovative projects can be difficult as time, or lack of it, is generally a factor that can make learning something new seem impossible. Learning the basics (and that is all you will need initially) about Podcasting only takes a moment of your time. Get inspired!

Finding excellent resources that can provide us with a cutting-edge approach to education and our individual subjects can be quite challenging at times.

JOURNALS

Most subjects have their own journal that contains new ideas about teaching and how to adapt government strategies for the classroom. They also have ongoing discussions about particular issues in education and specific topics. Subscribing to one of these is a must for any classroom practitioner who wishes to stay ahead in education and receive ideas that can assist his or her own teaching.

ONLINE

They are hundreds of sites that offer guidance and support for teachers, whether new to the profession or experienced. Some of these focus on providing articles about key topics or general information about various aspects of pedagogy. Many companies nowadays also offer online courses that teachers can sign up to, particularly courses about the use of ICT in various subject areas. These are generally of good quality as they are short, concise and, most of the time, provide the participant with additional resources at the end of the course. As they take place online, they are often very cheap and you can sit with a nice cup of tea, your feet up and your computer in your lap!

A relatively new resource that has become popular among new teachers is live online seminars and conferences. You sign up via the site and pay the fee, which is a fraction of the price you would normally pay. This is a great way of keeping your subject knowledge up-to-date and moving your professional development in the right direction

Getting new ideas about teaching is easier than ever, thanks to the ever-growing global community. There are various interesting tools to use and they can all be adapted to your way of thinking.

EXPAND YOUR HORIZONS – GOOD LITERATURE AND COURSES

BE INNOVATIVE – TEACH YOURSELF SOMETHING NEW

Feeling that your teaching is becoming mundane and lifeless? Do not fear, for help is at hand. Try these new software packages and your teaching will be full of colour again!

DO SOMETHING INTERACTIVE – ADOBE CAPTIVATE

Captivate lets the user take charge and get creative instantly, and provides an opportunity for teachers and students to create interactive simulations and demonstrations effortlessly. Captivate automatically records all onscreen actions and instantly creates an interactive Flash simulation, which can easily be used in lessons or added to websites. You simply point and click to add text captions, narration, and e-learning interactions – and you don't need any programming knowledge. You can use this software for all subjects, and even create websites that your colleagues can update whenever they want to.

DO IT YOURSELF – CONTRIBUTE 3

This excellent programme lets you publish your resources quickly and easily on the web in three simple steps: browse to the page that needs updating, edit it, click 'publish', and it's done. This means that any member of the department can change the content and layout of the website immediately without any knowledge of html or various web building applications. In essence, teachers can edit and upload resources and information on the fly.

There are many programs out there that would be useful to education. However, these two are relatively cheap and are very easy to use. Most importantly, they can be used for all subjects.

Stuck for ideas or just want to talk to like-minded professionals about education? Then why not join an educational forum online? There are many good forums available for teachers nowadays and most of them require you to sign up using only your email. Here are a few ideas of what to think about when using forums.

BE CLEAR

When you submit your post (or 'thread' as it is sometimes referred to), make it clear in the subject heading what your post is about – otherwise you may never get a response.

DO YOUR RESEARCH

Before posting, make sure you use the search facility on the discussion board so that you do not post another message about 'When does term start?' or similar. The search facility is an excellent tool in general, as you can scroll through topics that you may find useful.

READ OTHER PEOPLE'S POSTS

If you find a message, or a topic, written by someone that you find particularly interesting, then click on their name and read other messages posted by that user. This facility is available on most good forums.

Giving teachers the opportunity to develop as professionals through training and meeting other colleagues who share similar sentiments about teaching can sometimes be difficult. One of the main obstacles is teacher workload. Joining a forum is an excellent way of by-passing this problem.

JOIN THE 'VIRTUAL' WORLD
(FORUM/DISCUSSION BOARDS)